T0193858

THE RISE AND FALL
OF THE GREAT
MOZAMBIQUE
AND MY ASIAN COMPASSION

• • •

The Forgotten

LALCRISHNA
ANUPCHANDRA

authorHOUSE®

AuthorHouse™
1663 Liberty Drive
Bloomington, IN 47403
www.authorhouse.com
Phone: 1 (800) 839-8640

Published by AuthorHouse   08/20/2015

ISBN: 978-1-5049-3327-8 (sc)
ISBN: 978-1-5049-3326-1 (e)

Library of Congress Control Number: 2015913669

Print information available on the last page.

Any people depicted in stock imagery provided by Thinkstock are models, and such images are being used for illustrative purposes only. Certain stock imagery © Thinkstock.

This book is printed on acid-free paper.

CHAPTER ONE

• • •

IN THIS FAST CHANGING WORLD, I find myself lost. I have lived in many countries and learnt about many cultures. I believe in God, I believe there is a meaning for why and who I am, but I feel lost. The overwhelming sense of needing to know what my purpose in life is and where I need to focus––this is my quest, and this is my story so far, and I am hoping that in recounting my glorious past my future will unfold and reveal itself to me.

My name is Krishna. Does it sound Indian? It is. Very typical, but everyone calls me Chris––a sort of sweet way of knowing you. We love to go to the church and pray to 'Lord Krishna God'. There are many other gods the Indian people believe in. I myself was born the same day as Lord Krishna in the Gugurati calendar, which is slightly ahead of the English one.

What would you say if life just happened your way? Would there be excitement for you?

As you live every moment life brings new joys and sorrows and we get to enjoy new dreams and realities as it all happens around you, so we compromise and try to find balance, right? You get up each day and come across new challenges. Life––it's just one more day of excitement as we enjoy the sunrise and sunrays, as everyone around us tends to rush into the world of necessity, the material world, to fulfil their needs, right? I have learned if we have that will of achievement we end up winning as we go on, but there are always hurdles to be confronted––so never mind. I hear you say, here we go again with that belief system or state of mind we call faith, right? Or shall we say we believe we are always working towards our needs and will always end up doing something positive, as there is no end to a new start–– because if we fail to achieve our goals, what stops us from trying again? Or shall we ask if we are winning? Seriously, life is a big game! I don't know, but I just make a positive decision so it will be a help as I keep trying to make the most of what I can; I believe that if you make positive decisions, you will make a difference, as you always need to make a decision, and life is based on a series of good decisions. Everything comes down to this––it's all just a big decision.

Indian people, or any other people, I think, do feel the same as you, as I have all the same needs or beliefs; but I believe that nature informs our importance, as we have to make a mostly wise and understanding move to get ahead in a positive way——but how, why and whether we should or can is another matter.

I really would describe myself as someone quite lost and confused in this area, but in this fast changing world of today anyone can easily fall prey to all the confusions of how to behave and how to please other people.

Every day I believe there is always someone above us guiding our way, no matter what we do or don't, because when we do it right we feel happy and when we fail, somehow it hurts, right? So would you say experience is important but making a wise decision is much more important?

Right, then if I talk about myself, maybe I will be boring because I'm just a man that makes a living by feeding people selling curry and rice in an Indian restaurant in Bracknell, and I like to make sure I enjoy it as much as my customers do——because life is all about enjoying yourself somehow, and I believe that by doing that right you really are staying on top of it all, in control; but I like to think positively, and have a sense of self-knowledge, or self-worth; while this is important, I also need to ask if anyone else can do a better job, and accept that maybe I can be wrong.

I am quite positive about every aspect of my life most times, as I like to do many things, live and experience life to the full, as I love to dream, think, talk a lot if I can, as well as read, write, listen. Listening to music is important for me because it makes me feel alive. Awareness of life is a creative energy——I love the sunrise in the morning, I enjoy the daylight, while moonlight is something I really treasure. I love the smell of the wind. Even in sleep there is the sense of fulfilment, of life in affirmation in a state of rest. I enjoy my sleep for then I am refreshed in the mornings for more everyday business and a rewarding workload.

I love rain and sun and snow in the winter, I love flowers and bees, I like a beer, and a bit of wine as well. I like women and their stylish ways, I love peace and quiet, I love food––and more food! I like the movies and popcorn, not forgetting the ice-cream! I like shopping and a bit of a laugh and fun and dancing, maybe singing when tipsy, and I enjoy walking and running––all important to me. Awareness of and some involvement in politics also makes for a balanced sense of responsibility. I like to make love, like to be respected and I respect other people. In other words, I love being alive––and like to *feel* alive, physically and psychologically. That's why I like boxing and football, a bit of occasional porn, and enjoy meeting friends and family. I have an adventurous spirit, so occasionally I like to bet on horses and sometimes the roulette, and like to drive myself everywhere. I love to go to the pubs and nightclubs for fun. I really do like the old computer and the gadgets, and so on and on. As I said, I love to live life to the full!

CHAPTER TWO

• • •

SOMETIMES IN LIFE there are people that have a chance to see the world. I am certainly one of those, as is probably obvious by now! I have had a chance to travel quite a lot in my life, but then, what is life without fun and new experiences?

I have enjoyed some wildly exciting days at Guiquindo Lodge in Inhambane, in Guinjata, under huge palms with 179 degrees of panoramic sea views and glorious sunrises, complete with spectacular long-distance views of whale's tales. Guiquindo Lodge is an upmarket Lodge in Guinjata with free-standing double bed units, all en-suite, and there are lovely sumptuous sofas and really romantic settings under the huge palm trees; there are also excellent facilities such as indoor and outdoor showers and corner baths. The Lodge boasts a huge central main kitchen area, with dining facilities and games area. The Portuguese-style beach bar and restaurant is a big attraction for people like me, always hungry with a choice of exquisite seafood––quite pricey but good value for money. There is also a great bar and TV. The expansive lighthouse reef near Pandanie is set amidst breathtaking beauty. The shops nearby include a bakery, bottle store, butchery and general dealers supplying a wide range of groceries. I had an exhilarating day there with some friends and we got really busy with everyone enjoying different activities, like hiking, fishing, kayaking, scuba diving, snorkelling, star-gazing, surfing, swimming, whale watching, windsurfing, scuba diving, fishing, canoeing, deep sea fishing, saltwater paddling, sea kayaking, ocean seafaring and really exciting horse riding.

I find there is so much to do that I usually just opt for snorkelling the coral gardens––my favourite pastime––and the diving has been described as the best in the world with awesome sightings of manta rays that come there mostly to give birth. Then there are hundreds of reef fish, lion fish, cuttlefish, stone fish, a multitude of eels, shrimps, crayfish, octopus, nudi branches and gardens of soft and hard corals.

What I really love are the chalets, luxury units exclusively built on the model of the private game reserves, complete with designer face bricks, huge sliding doors and windows allowing perfect panoramic views of the sea.

I love to use the dhow from Inhambane to Maxixe, and if you take the diving in these waters they are the best sea safaris in the world. You can see the whale sharks, turtles and whales. The expansive blue sea is always a reminder of how life can be in this location with its glorious beaches, fantastic weather, splendid seafood and the friendly locals where lots of people have a relaxing holiday in my unforgettable land of Mozambique. What an experience!

Life has changed for me since I left Africa, some time ago now, as I have become used to the European lifestyle with all its comforts. Life is as exciting as you make it. I love living in a comfortable way, but like everyone else I find it can be a struggle each day, for each day brings its own joys and sorrows. I have certainly experienced difficulties adapting to and making headway in the English way of life, but now after years of hard work things are better; still, every day brings its own challenges and new experiences, since, whether at work or home, change is constantly taking place at an increasing pace. I am always trying to keep on top of things, to come out the winner, for one has constantly to adapt to the demanding lifestyle one is inadvertently caught up in in the western world. In my case it's like facing one challenge after another—maybe that's called living life in the fast lane with its changing facts and needs! In all this I have come to learn the importance of one big thing: just take it easy and go forward as positively as possible and with the determination to somehow see your way through it all.

CHAPTER THREE

· · ·

WORKING IN A CURRY HOUSE can be hectic. It seems I am always rushing around and in effect running the show, being responsible for the shopping and organising the restaurant and the staff, ensuring the restaurant is always clean and tidy, and at the same time always trying to smile. The customers are always in need of attention so being alert is important; every day you have to make sure you have enough stock of food and drink, as there is always something in need or in danger of being in short supply. Disaster is averted by thinking and planning ahead, and being constantly organised and on your toes. Ensuring that my restaurant serves the best Indian food around is something I enjoy doing; I have observed that a good many people love the chilli hot dishes, so in this area I have kept abreast of demand and tastes, confident that I can make a difference by always checking the chefs are pulling their weight and doing the job right, that quality is maintained, and that the food is unique to my restaurant, always up to scratch.

When you are working every day, life most of the time can be a challenge and I believe that hard work always pays— but it needs that extra effort for a person to achieve what he or she strives to be. I believe that your path through life is already there, already prepared for you to follow. No matter what you do or don't, life in a sense mostly drives itself along the lines of your destiny. Some are luckier than others when it comes to destiny. Maybe it's just a matter of what is there for you to live for or maybe dream about in the first place. Material things are important, but above it all, I believe in happiness and self-respect. A good education can shape your destiny for it can be very crucial in challenging today's world; with fast-changing laws and ideas, needs can vary much more with times. I do have to say that change is important, for it affects the needs that drive me forward, to maybe have a better day and above all a better life; as you win, lose or accept a challenge, what is life all about? Run, run blindly to keep up with change and live a life of stress? Or take it easy and live longer? Or just go with the flow as life goes forward? Or just feel sorry for yourself? Be positive, I believe!

This takes my mind back to the war I witnessed in Mozambique in my childhood, which required one to adapt or die. The effects of the war, as I said before, live with me. The memories still haunt me for it is still in my mind how brutal this civil war was, maybe one of the most brutal conflicts ever waged in Africa. I think it lasted 16 years, and hunger, disease and violence were the effect, and millions more were forced to flee their homes to different parts of the country while lots more escaped to neighbouring countries as the schools and hospitals were burned and the industries left in ruins with landmines buried throughout the land––landmines that claimed many victims over the years, including civilians like women and children. It was quite an era.

During the time that I was growing up in Mozambique, the civil war was a constant companion. Every day there was some kind of bad news around and about people living in bad conditions. The ruling party FRELIMO (Front for the Liberation of Mozambique) was founded in 1962 to fight for the independence of the Portuguese Overseas Province of Mozambique. The civil war began in 1977 when FRELIMO was violently opposed by RENAMO (the Mozambique National Resistance movement), an anti-Communist political faction sponsored by the white minority governments of the then Rhodesia and South Africa. I was very small then, 7 years old, and over 800 thousand or more died in the fighting and as a result of starvation. Five to six million civilians were displaced and many caught by landmines were made amputees. It all ended around 1992 and got better after that, but it was a time when I witnessed all the dreadful happenings, like the killings, shootings, executions, forced starvations, beatings to death and so on––but I guess it's all part of war, and I really did not understand a lot then; now however it's quite clear why, but it's something that lives with you. Now, happily, things have changed and I really like all the prosperity the country has achieved over the years since 1992.

As I grew up on the roads of Mozambique my impressions of the people and the land were always based on just what I could see around me; but the reality is placed in a better perspective when you travel the world, for then you experience other ways of life and the differences in the lifestyles in different countries––all of which seem far removed from that of my childhood. I am certainly very fortunate in having seen and experienced the war-torn life in Mozambique with its sufferings, from the intimate perspective of life on the roads of Africa, the fight against the illnesses; it's quite a challenge to the mind, for if you visited the country itself, you would find it can be inspiring, heart wrenching, saddening or maybe humbling, all at the same time. I said I was fortunate to have experienced or witnessed this, because it would be hard to describe all these mixed feelings, as daily life presents the recurring images of deprivation and is what you see all around you, the things a little boy who walks the street with a goat would see––the children eating food out of the rubbish bins on the side of the road, the *mamanas* (mothers, women) that carry huge kettles of water on their heads, people who are dancing and singing near the road, elderly women or men who are carrying huge loads of branches on their heads and backs, and maybe children without legs or arms begging for money, and people with no clothes, just with a few shreds of cloth on. As we all are aware, there were and still are all sorts of diseases present, HIV being the hardest to tackle, and AIDS or STDS (sexually transmitted diseases); but then the people are always smiling in spite of the malnutrition and the cholera or any other of the diseases that lurk on their doorsteps. It's just matter of survival, I guess!

I witnessed the war at close quarters in my childhood, as well as the effects of the war, so like I said, it all lives with me and is still in my mind as I recall just how brutal this civil war was––maybe one of the most brutal conflicts ever waged in Africa, and, as I said, I think it lasted 16 years. Hunger, disease and violence was the consequence and the order of the day, and millions more were forced to flee their homes to different parts of the country and further afield.

Chapter Four

• • •

I WAS BORN into an Indian family and, as you know, the Indians, on every corner they find, will open a shop! So it was an obvious choice for my Dad who did exactly that! This meant he could support a large family of nine, of which I am the oldest son and therefore I had to be successful; this was never in doubt—it was taken for granted and it was expected.

Mozambique as you know is an interesting country with not a large population but rapidly growing, where the people are maybe more passive; but with fast political changes its prosperity is quite surprisingly fast. We as former citizens who were born in the country do not really 'feel' any different, but the longer I live in England I become less aware of the past and perhaps have lost track of it all.

Alter the war, as I lived through the rest of my childhood in the south of the country of my dreams, nature always brought new surprises and different adventures; there was always someone getting married or having a magnificent style of honeymoon in the best destination available, where the sun-drenched beaches are always packed with tourists from around the African nations or the world—as people love to find exotic spots for their special occasions.

Mozambique offers those lovely destination spots, the spots couples think of for honeymoons and weddings; the hotels and the people there specialise in the catering and organising of these types of events and are always ready to help; they arrange blessing ceremonies, guest accommodation, wedding breakfasts, lunches or dinners, not forgetting the photographers and the special needs for that special long-awaited and dreamed of honeymoon.

There are so many islands that offer an exquisite degree of comfort, like Matemo, Medjumbe, Quilalea, Vamizi in the Quirimba Archipelago, Ibo, Bazaruto Island, Benguerra Island, Bazaruto Archipelago, Ilha de Mocambique in Nampula. There are other smaller places as well, quite special, along the coast like Pomene, Beline and Chidenguele. There are also the cruise ships that I love so much, as they offer all the luxuries you will find in hotels, like the big South African ship that plies the waters—stunning, providing top class service; these always welcome you and offer the same impeccable service as those top class meals are served in the comfort of your cabin. Their facilities are dedicated to your health and wellbeing, to make your life while on board enjoyable, ensuring your dream holiday comes true.

Staying at Villa N'Banga, which provides self-catering accommodation in Bilene, is quite special. Few of my friends had a more memorable time than staying at this villa, a safe and secure environment with night watchman patrolling the area, and just ten minutes from the ocean, as the villa is so stunning with the best garden views imaginable. There are also cosy bars with special facilities for cocktails and nice views of the sunset. It is a perfect location for weddings with an agreeable restaurant with lots of palm trees around.

While at sea in the big boat––a ship, really!––I noticed these beautiful creatures swimming alongside! When I looked closely it appeared they were smiling at me as they gracefully kept pace with the ship, jumping and then disappearing into the seawater, then surfacing again, all the time making those funny noises! They looked so funny and there are no words to describe them! These beautiful creatures with their graceful smiles are, of course, dolphins, and we humans find them enchanting: they are so intelligent and the tumbling ocean waves make them look so stunning and graceful under that hot sun. These mammals are mostly found in aquatic surroundings, some in rivers as well. I found them so special that I just kept looking at them, fascinated, for hours while travelling on the ocean near Tofo Beach.

The weather is always hot for most of the year, the plantations always fertile where we or the local people call Machamba. I was born in a bay of the town of Inhambane. My local dialect is Bitonga but I have now lost the language due to my travels at such an early age. The waters of that bay were the best part of my life, and from anywhere in the world

I can always picture the scene; as the blue reflections hit my face, they cast a spell on me as I watched, entranced, looking far into the horizon. It's something that I can never describe in written words, but anyone with the right frame of mind would understand me quite perfectly. People of Africa, meaning people from Africa, have the will and power for always wanting to make something of themselves; not surprisingly I grew up constantly with that need, that desire, of learning a little bit more, but not having the chance of carrying on with my education that any of us needed in the changing times and always with poverty at your door, the yearning remained unfulfilled––always feeling helpless to help and never being able to lift myself out of this situation, for politics was always the biggest hurdle of all. In my times at least my Dad could provide an adequate education with a chance of succeeding at secondary school, when the civil war was one of the biggest problems, malaria being a close second. People with luck like me did have a chance to make something of themselves, however, whereas the less fortunate just had to stay and work for those fractional wages that the government provided. My wife has a real Indian education and I admire her for that.

CHAPTER FIVE

• • •

MY MUM taught me from an early age the ways of the Indian culture, the gatherings that the Indian people follow and I learned quite a lot of the way Indian people like to dance. The Nawratri is a nine-day festival that people around the world enjoy; all the Indians get together to dance and pray for nine consecutive days: it's called Garba in our language. You see the way people take pride in their dress—it's quite amazing. I always had to look smart, which made my Mum very proud. Mum knew how to sing all the songs and get people dancing as well. I always found it mesmerizing and really enjoyed singing and dancing amongst those stylish, colourful sari dresses that she loved to wear so much, and how beautiful she always looked! Garba is a way Indian people get together and pray to a goddess for the betterment of their lives, and, if I'm not mistaken, for the wellbeing of the people. It lasts through the night, dancing, followed by a prayer, and afterwards you get *prasad* (sweets) and fruits as well. The children, as well as the old, love to dance. The festival of lights is quite famous for celebrating the end and beginning of a new year, where the power of lights engenders such a supreme feeling! It's the way it's commemorated all around the world. All Indian rituals have a meaning and I don't really understand much of it all, but having a wife with strong Indian beliefs is something I have been blessed with in my life.

As the year goes by Indian culture has become involved in all types of activity and it's pleasantly surprising that an Indian lady needs no excuse and will always get involved in prayers. I am a believer of all the powers up there, but we must have a lot of ways of praying and lots of time different chants, for indeed we all have different images of God.

We have our ways taught to us by our ancestors and it's a way to keep following what and where they come from back in that huge country called India. Did you know that our people acknowledge a serious amount of dialects and idioms? Hundreds, I think, but everyone speaks Indi (ardu) as it's an international language.

Whenever we could we travelled, for we loved to travel. We always ended up crossing a river and we loved to stop to view the flow of the water as well as people, as people were travelling in their boats up and down stream. The Mozambican rivers are quite clean because there is not much pollution in the country of my dreams, as *Rio* (means river) Limpopo is quite exceptionally big; but there are lots of other rivers in the country as we learned in our schooldays: Rio Rovuma, Rio Save, Rio Shire, Rio Zambezi, Rio

Pugne, Rio Mwenezi, Rio Mazowe, Rio Manyame, Rio Buzi, Rio Chinde, Rio Komati and River Maputo, where, as we witnessed lots of times, flooding is something that quite often happens in some areas, though it's not surprising when it does turn around, when the slow-running stream can cause serious damage; but even with all these problems, people love to live near the rivers, mainly for food, transport, water and protection.

Flooding can bring destruction to food crops and food shortages and even starvation in some areas. Large scale destruction happens as well in certain areas, as I have witnessed regarding the River Limpopo. In the main, however, the river can be so pleasant and it brings peace and tranquillity, as floods are Mother Nature's natural events and mainly happen in river catchment areas. The rivers in Africa are stunning to look at, and provide so many animals with their livelihood, as well as supporting the natural vegetation. I love the rivers.

I think it was in school that I learned that Mozambique is a fertile and unexplored country, as the coastline stretches for around 2500 kilometres with the Indian Ocean alongside. The economy growing at a fast rate with the infrastructure being sorted with better political stability, the future looks promising. There have been few setbacks such as earthquakes, though there have certainly been droughts and flooding. Extreme poverty unfortunately remains widespread, as over half of the population does not have the facilities of safe water and, with inadequate sanitation, there are water related illnesses like diarrhoea. Today there are water aids with better sanitation and hygiene education, as affordable technology is now more available to the people as the families and the children have a chance of improved health, which in turn may well lift them out of extreme poverty. There is a lot of government help and foreign aid workers are changing the infrastructure to provide safer and possibly better and more affordable ways of life.

On the continent of Africa, especially in Mozambique, the children are already poor and uneducated and wars and famine have brought more miseries as families got misplaced as people got driven away from their homes to foreign lands as refugees; parents lost their children and vice versa and they got abandoned with no one to care for them as they then become the street kids who had no choice but to live with little food and fend for themselves. There is lots of support now but it's a huge necessity to get everyone educated and out of poverty.

CHAPTER SIX

• • •

ON SUNDAYS I loved to go on safari with a friend of mine and his dad. Life used to be fun. "Let's take a day off on Sunday," my Dad would suggest, "early morning!" On the day I heard my Dad shouting for me. All I could hear was that someone was supposed to get up, but did not realise it was me! Friends had come to pick me up and little did I know, then, that I was on the way to the best day of my life, to a safari park to see the animals. Have you ever seen the *real* animals wandering around you? I have and it's good fun!

Mozambique offers an extensive wilderness area for the safaris, and the one we went to while we lived there was the Gorongosa National Park in the heart of Mozambique. It's really big, I think over three thousand square kilometres, with seasonal flooding and waterlogging of the valley, and grassland dotted with acacia trees and savannah; dry forests abound on sands and there are seasonal rain-filled plains and termite hill thickets, the plateau containing Miombo and Montane forests and a spectacular rainforest. It does have quite a dense wild life population, typical of this area of Africa, which includes lion, elephant, hippos, zebra, wildebeests, waterbuck, impala, black rhino, all of these concentrated by the water along the riverbanks of the Vundudzi River and other small rivers around. The buffalo I think were the best to see while eating; the colours that these animals have is just beyond description! It's just superb, and when you are so close to them it's just out of this world. Wild life I think is the one thing I would recommend to whoever loves animals and the African ones are just fantastic to see.

As we went around that day, the park seemed to be enormous. I think we travelled quite a distance, bearing in mind that the park covers more than three and a half thousand square kilometres in the great African rift valley that extends, I believe, from Ethiopia to near central Mozambique. African life is quite fascinating and different as the people are very friendly. In a way I was spoilt for choice when it came to having a chance to live life in the African way; education is something that really helps and I and lots of my little friends had the opportunity to learn, live and enjoy the Inhambane way of life to the full; as they say thank you in their language: *khanimambo!* It was a blessing to feel and live the reality of life in Africa.

Gorongosa Park is home to an astounding diversity of animals and plants, from small insects to large mammals; in this area alone there must be four hundred types of birds as well as a big variety of reptiles. Gorongosa Mountain and National Park near Beira and the border of Zimbabwe comprises 1-2 million hectares of open bush, swamp and waterways, spread between the rivers Urema and Pugne. I think what I really enjoyed about that day was to see the zebra with their white stripes and, as you know, they are vegetarians, so it was superb to see them eat and just wander about and keep eating and walking.

Safaris are good days out, but be prepared, it can be quite a tiring day and never forget to take along a bottle of water! Don't forget your camera, too, to have all your memories recorded.

CHAPTER SEVEN

• • •

REALLY, sometimes I feel lost and it's so hard to adjust to life's daily changes; life can be stressful on account of the demands to live a good life and pay your way, always maintaining a decent code of life and scale of values. There are times when it feels as though my life is always work, work and work! Although I have been around the world and enjoyed myself somehow, I find another day brings another history, but with this fast-changing world I think the way for me to lead to common-sense and new horizons, is to keep trying new things and succeed in what I attempt, taking one step at a time. What really helps me to keep pace with these continuing challenges, however, is knowing when to rest and recuperate. I love to take a boat sometimes down the Thames river near Windsor, cruise away downstream and enjoy a pint of Carling Beer and maybe a snack, and just chill out, daydream and watch the people around me throwing bread crumbs to the ducks and white swans with their lovely long necks. I enjoy doing the same––it's fun throwing bread at them! Sometimes I also like to enjoy an ice-cream cone, which is quite cheap to buy. Perhaps that little breeze on your face makes you forget all the stress of everyday life as you just relax and have a wonderful carefree afternoon! What I am saying is, is that the element of fun is an essential part of life! Fun enhances your coping skills, and indeed we cannot have a healthy life without it.

Have you ever had to make life decisions? I ask this because I have to make decisions all the time––at home, at work and in personal ways as well. I think it's the most difficult thing a person does in life––taking or making a decision! Making a choice as well is a big decision, trying to say yes or no is a big decision; life itself is a decision, to do something or not is a decision, to buy something expensive (or not) is a decision, or have a cheaper version is a decision; being positive is a big yes, or affirmation!

When presented with choice, if you take a decision the responsible way is surely the right decision. Being happy is the right way too, I guess. There is one thing that I learned from my mum, and that is the need to cultivate a healthy eating habit. She loves to cook fresh food normally, but there are some choices at home, like having less meat, and grilled rather than fried; and she likes more poultry and fish instead of high fat foods like sausages, frankfurters and bologna, and any form of processed meat is out! She uses less butter, ice-cream, cheese, cream and more of semi-skimmed milk and very often I notice she loves low fat products like skimmed milk, yogurt and cottage cheese. We used to have eggs but not a lot, and commercial biscuits and cakes, only sometimes for special occasions. She loves to cook with olive oil, soya and corn, and to look after the teeth she would not let as have much sweets; she approved, rather, of fruit, not forgetting vegetables like peas and beans. For breakfast we loved and were allowed wholemeal bread and cereals. It's something that you might have once, and enjoy, as we did, and before long we got used to it as a regular routine. It works, for me especially, because I became diabetic and consequently I need to watch my sugar level.

CHAPTER EIGHT

• • •

COMING BACK TO AFRICA, Inhambane, as I said before, is a wilderness district, as well as a town where all sorts of businesses take place. The people there are the most relaxed I have ever met. Going around the world, you find there is nothing that changes the feeling of very friendly people, who are relaxed and secure in their disposition. Vasgo da Gama was a sailor, a Portuguese explorer who, in colonial times, called the people of this region *'terra de boa gente e ma lingua'*, which means 'nice people but with the bad habit of gossiping, though generous at heart'––and it will always be that way, though the people now are much more modern with their TV, computers, and all the gadgets that are now being sold at a fraction of the original price. The local people have moved to a more modern way of life but have always kept that sense of wellbeing, knowing who and what they are rather than trying to be any other culture. I know the people of Inhambane by the shorter name, I'BANE. The town is my Mother's unforgettable town of birth, and for her it is and always will be the best!

As I'm telling you more about the people, it comes to mind that they all are very much into respectable dresses, men always wearing shirts and trousers while the women wear Kapulana, and are as beautiful and colourful as you can imagine. Kapulanas are very colourful, long designer clothes that the local woman there love to wear. They can make 'sais', which means maxis they can wind around the waist or roll on the top the heads; wearing these, they just look fabulous and attractive, and that local 'feel' you sense, seeing them, never goes away as you get so used to it as you live longer and longer with the people; but always remember, the country is located in the South East of Africa, where the weather tends to be hot, so hot that you need to cover yourself somehow. The local people are used to the climate where, being part of the South Tropics, the weather is always humid or very hot. In this climate you would love to survive on the beer––and indeed, people like me are always ready for one anytime!

The local beer is called 2M and we jokingly say 'dois malucos', which means 'two crazy souls', and I must say it's quite a brew, as everyone always loves a sip of it! My local friends are always ready for drinking adventures that we always love to have around the town whenever the chance presents itself. Another brand of beer is called Laurentina; there are so many beers and you start discovering more and more choices as you check the shelves of the local shops. Variety is something that never ends because the people of the town are always looking for fun for some reason. Inhambane is and always will be the town that gives me the most memorable times, over and over again; it will surely do the same for you, any time you go there, live there or just remember it from afar, like I do!

As the days go by, the markets get quite busy, as the people have to do their shopping. The locals really are quite fussy though not always so fussy as you might expect, since you will always meet some with different ideas of what to cook today or tonight!

When I was on a holiday last September to see my parents and the extended family, we experienced a traditional ritual of *sapta,* where everyone meets to pray for their ancestors. I used to love to wander around the market with my Mum or anyone of the house who was up to a bit of shopping. I always loved to see the *tarbuth,* the local melon, green and with that red inside look of the juices that are lovely to eat and quite refreshing. The *papaya,* another local fruit, is very famous; then there is *manga,* which means mango, and *ananas,* which means pineapple; also tangerines, oranges, tamarind––the list goes on and on. I really loved the way those *mamanas,* the local trade ladies, do business with the foreigners; you will get a bargain if you start by asking around how much it would cost, then just moving on, asking again until you find the best product and obviously the best price. It can be quite an experience learning how it all works, taking care not to give your money away. I think that my Mum is a very good, experienced buyer, as I watched and learned from her, wandering around with her.

Looking back I think, now, that every time you go shopping it is a new experience.

In Africa, especially in Inhambane, I find that everything we buy in the markets is quite fresh, from fish to meat, from crabs to vegetables, from bread to any Indian food the locals love. My town's *bissi bissi* can be the best: it's normally cooked with coconut sauce, onion gravy, not forgetting the small sun-dried little prawns in the shell. I tell you, it's quite a mouth-watering dish!

The juice makers are always here and there, but I find that local people love their *thonthonto*––the quite powerful and smelly local *feny*, alcohol, that the older men love to drink while relaxing or eating. It's a way of local life that I find quite interesting, depending on how you mix with them and enjoy their way of life. This brew can have a cashew nut, peanut or tangerine flavour, and is something everyone should try! Do you know that *thonthontos* in the traditional culture of the region are used to help people in medicine, some mixing it with honey to create so-called hot toddies in England. It's quite helpful to see how the traditional ideas do work, as well as used or implemented in cooking as well.

The plantations on the land, nearer the small rural towns as you drive away from the town of I'Bane, constitute what you would call the most spectacular view ever to be seen, a view that someone like me always admires. I think the banana plantations are quite a sight when seen in the nearer distance; that green calm feeling you get when seeing the plantations and the surroundings terrain from far off I find quite a sublime experience.

'Massaroca, ya ya yam'––that is something I love to see: the corn fields! The Mozambican people love to eat all the *macaroca* corn in a way that you really feel the local difference, which makes you want to stop for a while and take a break for whatever reason. On the side of the roads people will sell them to you. When they are grilled and served with butter, they seem to provide the palate with an altogether different and delicious experience. Some love to eat corn on the cob with salt and others with a bit of chilli flavour.

CHAPTER NINE

• • •

IN THE REAL WORLD we wake up in the morning and always have to crack on with our personal duties and necessities. I wonder at such times if everything we do makes sense or not! I sometimes wonder, but there is someone up there guiding us to the end of the tunnel to see the light; you plod along and make another goal, maybe win or maybe lose. One might think at the time it's just another day gone by, but past experiences make one more aware of not making the same mistake twice. Nevertheless, one plods on regardless!

Sometimes stress can lead to headaches. I learnt that Indian massages are the best antidote for this, like the head massage which is quite popular; indeed, I think it is wonderful and can be relaxing, especially where the massage includes the shoulders, neck, upper back, head and face, for it's a holistic therapy that somehow balances the body and mind and spirit and promotes a sense of wellbeing and, most importantly, your health—especially as the stress of modern life, poor diet and the fast-paced lifestyle, as well as pollution can unbalance and block our energy.

There are so many different Indian drinks that I love, like *nimbu pani,* orange smoothie, pistachio shake, spiced tea, strawberry shake, *tarbooj sharbat, thandaai, khus ka sharbat, badam ka sharbat, anar ka sharbat* pineapple shake, *chickoo* shake, litchi shake, golden shake, cola shake, cold coffee, ginger fruit punch, *gulab sharbat, jeera lassi, kharbhooja sharbat,* mango lassi, *meethi* lassi, ginger ale, apple shake, *kesar badam* shake, *chandan ka sharbat,* chocolate shake, cardamom shake, basil tea, banana shake, banana lassi, *angoor sharbat,* almond honey milk and *aam panna.* These are quite famous, and popular with Indian people and very much enjoyed worldwide, but mostly in India. I have tried lots or almost all of them. It's fun having different drinks.

The head massage originates from the eastern part of India, going back in time thousands of years. It all runs in traditional Indian families and was developed as a grooming technique by the women, to help strengthen and improve the fullness of the hair as part of everyday life. It is referred to by the Indian word *champissage (champi* means 'massage' in Indian). Although Indian head massage is part of Indian family life, traditionally it spreads outside to the market places, street corners and barbers' shops.

Oil is used to promote healthy hair growth, shine and heal scalp conditions with various herbs and spices, and it helps slow down the greying process. The *yurvedic* healing system is quite famous.

Indian head massage is beneficial for stress-related symptoms like tension headaches, muscle aches and pains, neck stiffness, sinus problems and insomnia. I find it all a help whenever I need it, as it gives me a wonderful sense of peace and relaxation and most importantly, tranquillity. The types of oils I use are grape seed oil, coconut oil and occasionally, sesame oil, jasmine oil and almond oil.

CHAPTER TEN

• • •

BACK WHERE I COME FROM, I had quite a different experience because of being born into an Indian family and educated in a Portuguese school, because it used to be a Portuguese colony. I grew up living in the midst of the traditional local Inhambane coloured people who were very friendly and helpful, and had to adjust to different needs because of the civil war. Thinking back to 1988, I had to share a three-bedroomed flat with a family of nine people and, in addition, had to come to terms with having to live with asthma and breathing problems; despite all this I had a wonderful childhood and cannot complain; instead, I cherish my memories that I will never forget. No matter what happens, memories of past times live with you, and I was always moving on to learn new things that life gave me the opportunity to experience; so I must have made the most of it, I believe; my childhood must have been one of the best, with no regrets or doubts whatsoever. Altogether, my childhood memories are of an unforgettable time that I shall always treasure.

God does comprise a big part of our lives. In our culture you get to eat all the Indian sweets, especially cooked for the occasions that all of the Asian community will find enjoyable; you get *barfis* made of milk and *pendas,* another version, *jalebis* that look like round oranges, *goolab jaman* which are quite sweet, *ganthias* and Bombay mix, and so on.

As time marches on people have to move on in life, and at the age of seventeen I had to make a decision. I needed to find a job and with the help of my Dad I decided I should go to Europe, so I ended up in Portugal with my uncle who has lived there for quite a long time, in Lisbon, the capital city of Portugal. I started working in a Cash and Carry store and worked in Miratejo and Almada, parts of Lisbon, for one year; and so it was a new start to my career, learning and gaining experience of how to run the store. The hours that I worked and the pay I got were not what you would call very favourable, but in spite of this, it was nice to live in Lisbon with all the real Portuguese cooking and the way they dance the *Fados*––a traditional, very special dance that all Portuguese love and which is quite famous worldwide. I think that the way they cook as well is fantastic, because I love their Piri-Piri chicken––one of the best chicken flavours you can have, and the cakes are quite an experience; the Sagres beer and the so-called *chorico assado* (grilled sausage) is the national speciality, not forgetting the Macieira brandy.

I was able to go to Portugal because I have a Portuguese passport, and as you know, Mozambique used to be a Portuguese colony before 1975 when Mozambique became independent and changed government. When I came to England in 1990 I found myself immersed in a very different experience altogether; as you, the reader, live here, I don't have to explain the reality, but everyone lives a different life and I enjoy mine so much. I think the European way of life is a pleasant and agreeable way; it can be quite stressful at times but I have no complaints—that is what life is all about, right? The one thing I really enjoyed in Southern Portugal was the Algarve where the beaches are so relaxing and with that 'tourist' feel; with all those foreigners relaxing and enjoying the sun and the calm relaxed way that the locals offer to help, it's a very nice side of the country.

As I grew up in Inhambane, we learned a lot about the Portuguese and when you live with them in Portugal it's not much of a difference; but back in Mozambique I think they have been influenced a lot by living in accordance with their traditional habits or customs. The schoolteachers, some of them nuns, were considerably helpful in the way we were educated; all their ideas from the colonial era are still alive in some of my memories and every time you meet an old friend they will always remind you of those days, no matter how much time has gone by in your life.

The Portuguese language is not difficult but obviously you need some practice, as in any other language. Dona Marias and Dona Lauras and Dona Margaret and Senhor Joao and Senhor juliao are typical names Portuguese people call themselves, and they have that unique way of being the proud people of the Gal. I salute them as every time you meet someone you say, *"Bom dia senhor?"* (good morning) or *"Como esta senhor?"* (How are you, mister?).

It's nice to speak so many different languages. I have had to because of the needs of my new locals and the way life is today. We are always meeting different types of people all the time. One thing that I find different in Portugal is that they drive on the right-hand side of the road, whereas here in England we drive on the left; they use kilometres and we miles, they have *degraus* (degrees) and we use Fahrenheit; they measure in centimetres and we still (to some extent) measure by the foot! It's just a different way of life, the way they live in Portugal—it's a unique way and so different to ours.

As I said, the way I was brought up is quite surprisingly normal (to me, of course!) as everyone has their own unique experiences. I used to love to play a bit of everything, from football to volleyball and basketball, do a bit of swimming sometimes and go down to the church to pray.

As I started to grow up I was living an everyday life going to school and meeting all my friends. I was always left to choose different things to do, as my parents were always busy with the other four children. I was the eldest and left to really make my own way as I always seemed to be doing okay! My life has always been this way and I have no complaints; I am used to it, so when I went anywhere I always made the most of it.

As you know, I was born into an Indian family and the Indians have their way of doing everything in a special order. One thing I got used to is that we must pray first and believe what we want is attainable and try to achieve the hardest possible goal. I remember that while I was small my parents would ask me if I believed all the rituals that were performed and if it ever made any sense to me? As time goes by in life everything changes, as you know, and my memory, I think, has changed in perspective, but never mind—we will still remember the best and most meaningful of those past experiences. As I was growing up in the eighties all the young people my age used to go to more or less the same schools and thus acquired the same education, which was beneficial at the time. I grew up studying in Portuguese. I had a chance to learn some English at the same time; I never realised then how useful this would be to me until I moved here! We really did have some good times but at the same time, people grow older and we all got a good education and people from there are doing well in life; when I meet my friends it's a joy to know they are also doing well. Some of them have become businessman and others have got good jobs so they can support themselves and their families.

CHAPTER ELEVEN

. . .

LIFE BACK IN MOZAMBIQUE is still a struggle for a lot of people; many are growing up without a good education and are still dependent on aid agencies as well as Oxfam, the Red Cross and other organisations doing humanitarian help work that you still see around Africa. I find it's quite hard for some people, but then what can we do? Mozambique has moved on and now it has become quite a prosperous country with all the international support and financial progress; it now has good roads, proper lighting and clean water piping. With the entire national infrastructure being modernised, it is becoming in many respects today's ideal world to live in. There is a lot of foreign investment being poured in and I noticed during my visit last year that it has changed a great deal—indeed, I could hardly believe what I was seeing! The beaches are so nice and clean and the water so blue; you will never come across such beautiful colours that these shores offer, and as regards the local fishermen when at sea in their boats, it's just amazing to see how do they do all that fishing, storage, transporting and selling! The boats they use still have the appearance of the traditional boats I recall seeing as a child, which adds to the picturesque beauty of the scene. Seeing them, the old memories come flooding back; you close your eyes and see the big fish in front of you and the smell is there too––the smell and sights, of red fish, jellyfish, big tiger prawns, or serra, shark fish––just name it and they sell it there.

As you may know, fishing is an old tradition back in Inhambane. While I was in Barra beach we had the magnificent *lulas assadas* with Mac Mohan beer, 2M, and the chillies they provide can be quite an experience––all served with chips, salad, followed by ice-cream. You have to try the *massaroca*, corn roasted or grilled, and it just goes on with Martini Rosso or *aguaardente*, and then the cigars! Wearing just sandals on your feet is a good idea because it is so hot; you should not be wearing trousers, but shorts and maybe a T-shirt, with some advert on it––then just get into the chilled, relaxed holiday mood!

As I was saying, I have these Indian ideas of how influenced I have been by my parents; religion can have a strong effect on the way we behave and I am a strong believer in God, but feel we all are, somehow.

Throughout my childhood we used to go to different beaches all the time. Let's consider some around where we live in Inhambane. As you know, with the end of the civil war in Mozambique (I think this was around 1992), all the costs were transformed in top safari and beach destinations on the continent of Africa. We have, I think, world class beaches, interesting Portuguese-style food, friendly and down-to-earth people. Mozambique offers around I think more than 1,100 kilometres of coastline and it is a paradise for beach goers, sailors, divers, fisherman, with what I call a rich culture. We have the Flamingo Bay Water Lodge, Barra Lodge and Pomene Lodge.

Flamingo Bay Water Lodge is situated in the Inhambane area, 485 km north of Maputo, the capital of Mozambique, and the waters are crystal clear as it leads to the warm Indian Ocean. It is home to lots of flamingos, tropical fish and rare dugong and the sunsets are breathtaking. If you like water sports, horse riding, sightseeing, quad bikes, mangrove forests, scuba diving, catamaran yachts, dhow trips, charter boat fishing—you name it, we used to enjoy all of them all the time here—you will love this place!

As we used to go to Barra Lodge we observed that the traditional casitas are made of thatch, brick and reeds; these always give you a charming atmosphere. It must have a few of those houses called casitas, around 15 or more, and there are double and a few single beds with en-suite shower, toilets and hand basin available. The mosquito nets are always visible everywhere you look and the refreshments unforgettable. We also loved to go to Pomene Lodge, 605 km from Maputo, the capital city; it is sheltered from the sea and wind and for someone looking to go back to nature, this corner of nature's paradise is the answer: it really feels like a seaside paradise.

Inhambane does offer lots of fun, for when you start looking around this seaside resort, you will discover that once you're there, you don't want to know anything about the world from which you have come or where you live! It has a magical effect on you as soon as you arrive—those fresh coconut trees around just add that magic and the coconut water is so refreshing as well, and the inside of the coconut so delicious to eat.

As time advances I love to get involved in lots of new activities, and Indian dances are something I like as there is a wide diversity of dances, like folk and classical. Folk dances are like the famous *bangra* of the *punjabis, dandiya* and *garba* of *gujaraties, yakshagana* of *karnataka, dekhnni* of goa, *lavani* of *maharastra, bihu* of *assam, chhau* of *jharkhand* and *orissa* and the *ghoomar* of *rajasthan*. There are all the new ideas as the young people are always innovating as they interact with western ideas in their sitting rooms nowadays, thanks to TV. Sport is something I always enjoy and while on holyday in India I learnt that cricket is most popular; also hockey to some extent; then there are also the *kabaddi,* the *gillidanda,* not forgetting the *kho kho.* Southern Indian guys love *kuttiyum kolum* and the snake boat race, as they are the new generation. Nowadays kicking a football has become popular too, being a result of football becoming a world famous game.

Do you know that lots of my friends loved to go for their honeymoon to Rio Azul (Blue River)? The Rio Azul is located on the banks of the Govuro River in Mozambique, about 2 km from the river mouth—that is about 130 km north of Vilanculos. It is used for African safari venues along the Mozambique coast, where it has access to strong currents and deep water close to the beach. It really offers for the honeymoon-goers all the sights imaginable––watching the fish and the way all the locals tackle the fishing in different methods.

The birdlife in the Mangrove region is the most fascinating on account of the vibrant colours, the stunning beauty of the really clean beaches that no-one can ever imagine; when you just keep looking at that blue colour of the skyline and that never-ending feel of the blue sea, you will be overcome with the wonder of creation. At the time when my education demanded a lot of time, the fun of visiting such beauty never ceased. My friend's Dad used to have a Land Rover car and on Sunday we enjoyed the safari trips if we were lucky! Let's take the time we went to Azura, an unspoilt island within a national park with deserted beaches of pure white sand, sunny days, swaying palms, the turquoise water of that lovely sea. It is the country's perfect luxury eco-boutique retreat. With the way the locals built it, the pool having been designed to give some privacy, it provides wonderful, relaxing seclusion. With the cuisine and the vast range of activities and the last word in comfort, this retreat is second to none; you have a perfect fusion of indoor and outdoor space with footsteps from the beach; the spa offers yet another activity, something else to consider during your stay.

CHAPTER TWELVE

• • •

THE RAINFOREST in Mozambique is something of great interest to me. It's located in the northern part of the country. It's quite a recent discovery by the researchers, and is called Mount Mabu, being one of the most important finds in recent years. The scientists describe it as "pristine", and it is obviously protected by the local authorities on account of the many species of reptiles found there, which are new to many and have never seen before. It's the biggest rainforest in southern Africa.

I went to Malawi to help my brother get married in 2004. This was to be the first time I had witnessed Malaria, which my sisters caught whilst travelling. It's quite a slow process: you start feeling cold, tired and feverish and it was awful to witness, seeing my own sisters suffering in this way. I had to hospitalise them whilst still helping with my brother's wedding. The nurses used glucose to give back some strength to my sisters, and also used chloroquine to help kill the disease.

Malaria is common in Africa and *plasmodium falciparum* is the dangerous one that I know. It causes a lot of deaths in most parts of Africa, and takes the lives of millions and occurs in over one hundred countries. My sisters contracted Malaria from a bite of a Malaria-infected mosquito; the parasites go into the bloodstream and continue to grow for about a week. They travel to the liver and then grow and multiply, as they reach the red blood cells. You can feel the sickness from as early as eight days after the mosquito bite. The symptoms can be fever, headache, muscle aches, shaking chills, and tiredness. It is very dangerous if not promptly treated. There are different types so you must see the professionals. I think that Unicef are doing a great job helping the African people.

The country has a typical tropical climate, which means that the extensive coastal lands are hot and warm most of the year. It experiences a single rainy season at the time of high sun, when the inter-tropical belt of clouds and rainfall are from a southerly direction.

As I said before, Inhambane is the land where I grew up and I still enjoy the coastline so much, as it hosts a number of beaches that are really worth visiting, and the area around Tofo beach is where most travellers tend to stay as it is a picturesque fishing village that has experienced a tourism boom in recent years. There are miles of unspoilt beaches and the sea is the most beautiful I have ever experienced. I have lived through lovely times there that are still very much in my memories——memories full of carefree fun.

As I grew up my education carried on as I learned a lot about the country that I am naturally proud of. It's the Republic of Mozambique in South East Africa, with Tanzania to the North, Malawi and Zambia to the North West, Zimbabwe to the West, and Swaziland and South Africa to the South West. It became independent in 1975 and I lived during the civil war times from 1977 to 1992. When we had the chance my Dad would take us travelling from Inhambane. We travelled a lot on his business trips. We must have visited the whole of the country from Rovuma to Maputo. It has 10 provinces with Maputo as the capital and largest city, the provinces being Gaza, Inhambane, Sofala, Manica, Tete, Nampula, Zambezia, Cabo, Delgado and Niassa. It's drained by five principal rivers, the famous one being the river Zambezi. The four lakes are tourist attractions and my Dad loved the Niassa Lake, as I know from our frequent visits there. We visited the other lakes too——Cahora, Bassa, and Shirwa, all in the North.

As I mentioned before, the tropical weather is characterised by two seasons; one is wet, from October to March, and the other dry, from April to September. Rainfall is quite heavy along the coast and decreases South to North. Cyclones always happen during the wet season.

The Frelimo Party runs the country and the currency is called the Metical. The language we spoke was Portuguese, but there are different languages; Bantus for example spoke

Swahili, Makhuwa, Ndau, Shangaan and Sena, mostly by natural Mesticos. As a result of reforms thousands of small enterprises were privatised and sector liberalisation went the same way like telecommunication, energy, ports and railways as the incentives by the local government were made to increase revenues in the country. 45% of Macuas are found in the Zambezi province alone, numbering four million; the Thesena and Shona also live in the Zambezi valley; the Shangaan are more in the south of the country as are the Makonde, Tonga, Chopi, Swahili and Nguni including Zulu. A lot of Indian migrants live in the country, not forgetting the Arabs as well. Religion is an important part of the country, as the Christians, Muslims and Roman Catholics all have a part.

CHAPTER THIRTEEN

• • •

GETTING MARRIED made a significant change in my life, back in 1997, when I was introduced to the real 'feel' or sense of a real-life drama, as I got to take on new responsibilities. My wife is a typical Indian wife with her religious beliefs. She is very much into religion, as she is a typical Indian woman. As a result you might say that I have the real-life experience of living with the Indian religious and cultural ethos in my own home.

Things really changed 'big time' for me in England, where I love to be in touch with the bookies, staying in afternoons to hear the horse racing results. Betting I found to be a very relaxing pastime, a source of great fun. This was eventually largely forgotten after marriage, however, when home-making became a more important part of my life. Trying to be a good partner and devoted husband demanded its own time. In our marriage we were more into traditional foods, festivals and a different circle of friends, with what amounts to family meetings on days offs and whenever required. Besides trying to adjust to a busier work ethic, I was adjusting to a new lifestyle too, and had to become more into enjoying Bollywood movies than Hollywood movies, trying to adjust and enjoy an Indian side of life and, above all, be a very loyal husband, focused on a way of life that would prove to be a balanced lifestyle. In a sense I was enjoying the 'new me', for my altered lifestyle in a marital relationship was a new journey of self-discovery. I did not just have myself to please or think about now, so in a way I was discovering myself as I adjusted to the new changes; I was able to appreciate that my wife is very special, being a good and genuine Indian woman who takes life seriously. She appreciates the value of hard work, yet also the importance of fun, at the same time maintaining a very disciplined lifestyle in which, in a sense, you have to forget pubs, nightclubs, smoking places, and avoid noisy places and choose more family-type surroundings like restaurants and churches, and family venues suitable to the ideal world of the family. To be honest, it's nice, and you need to remember there are necessary choices to make, especially when you need a very loyal partner; so finding a sincere and disciplined partner was for the good. At the end of the day things really get done!

When I got married our honeymoon was in Tofo Beach. This is going back to 1997. One day we all went to Jangamo Beach Resort, and what a day it was! It is situated around 25km south of Inhambane, and it has lots of Portuguese heritage sites left from earlier times.

Praia de Jangamo has the deep blue sea on one side and big forests on the other, as a backdrop for the tourists who love the scuba diving. We were on the sand enjoying a picnic when some fishermen turned up with this lovely Garopa——a local fish, nice to eat and it looked so beautiful. It was all so enchanting, the Indian ocean with its panoramic views stretching ahead of us, and yet there was the convenience of all the facilities nearby, with food supplies, pharmacies, hospitals, restaurants as well as communication facilities. We always enjoyed the coconut trees and the activities around us; we were so excited and loved to sail in those blue waters; we had just the best Piri-Piri *galinha cafrial* that I still remember vividly; it was the best day ever and the chicken was superlative——the best I have enjoyed with the family members on that Jangamo shore.

As we had time every other Sunday, my friends would always have an excuse of finding places for enjoyment; we loved to go to the Prais de Tofo (beach), Praia dos Cocos, Ponto da Barra ilha de Banquera and the Guinjata Bay, and we loved swimming. These were the cleanest locations that I remember, where manta reef and scuba diving is quite popular in Gallaria. The marine life is just the best I have ever come across——we even saw a whale shark! We had seen some back in Tofo Beach and the big turtles and the giant manta rays, and don't forget the town of Maxixe is just across the bay. The trade is mostly cashew nuts, cotton and pearls. We used to love to travel to Maxixe by boat. It's fun, and I think it was named after an African chief. We would go to see the family and it was always a pleasure to do business there, as it's always been the busiest commercial town.

As we grew up my Dad bought a shop in Cumbana province and I used to sell and trade in *capulanas,* local dress, *farinha de mandioca, feijao* (beans), *cha preto* (tea), *assafrao,* and lots of other stuff that endlessly filled the shop with whatever the people of Cumbana needed. We loved to go shopping around the village and have all those fruit parties and try the local cooking, from *feijao soupa* (soup), *mathapa* (green leaves like spinach cooked with dried prawns), and *sura* (a juice that tastes nice and bit sweet, loved by the locals).

Have you ever heard of Arquipelagos? I loved to travel (any excuse would do!) and we invariably ended up going to Quirimba Arquipelago that stretches from Pemba to the Rovuma River which has more than 25 coral islands. You simply walk and walk and just walk, and at the end you have collected beautiful shells; the area has never been explored to the fullest extent––I think it's a tropical tourist paradise, and it's on the border of Tanzania and Mozambique. While there we had grilled *lulas assadas*––it was delicious, with some *ananas* fruit juice (pineapple juice) and *pao* (bread). My Dad loved to wander around in shorts and enjoy the breeze––it was a lovely day trip.

The products consist mostly of beverages, tobacco and obviously food, the big cities like Beira, Maputo, Matola and Nampula supplying a ready market. Mozambique's industrial sector produces raw material such as sugar, cashews, tea and wheat; brewing is important, as well as textile production, and fertilizers, cement, not forgetting agriculture. There is also the production of soaps, glass, oils, ceramic, paper, tires, radios, you name it. Major investments are steel, aluminium, mineral extractions, fertilizers and sugar productions.

The basic infrastructure like roads, bridges, schools, clinics has an impact on the growth of the country, but there are natural gas reserves offshore and onshore, and of course there is the agricultural industry––the natural livestock of animals, and plants.

CHAPTER FOURTEEN

• • •

THE MUSIC we love to hear back in my home country depends on what type of gathering you may be involved in. Take the Makonde, who love to do ritual dancing with wood carvings, and it can be accompanied by *shetani* (evil look), with evil spirits mostly curved from heavy ebony. There are so many varieties of music and dance. For example the Chopi love to show off with animal skin dresses and act as though in battle, and the men in Macua like to dress in colourful outfits and masks and dance away for hours and hours. All the musical instruments are handmade and the drums are made of wood and animal skin. The Lupembe is a woodwind instrument made of animal horns and wood. The Marimba is quite popular with the Chopi, performed with wonderful skill and the most accomplished dancing. It can be compared with a West Indian reggae. Mozambique people love *marrabenta,* and the *fado,* samba, and *kizomba.* The bitonga dance, which the locals used to dance when we have had friends for a party, is very lively.

I have talked about malaria, but there are so many other diseases that you must be aware of in Africa. I have come across a few, like yellow fever, polio, typhoid, tuberculosis, cholera, syphilis, malnutrition, hepatitis, HIV/AIDS, amebiasis, dengue, ebola, giardiasis, polio, hypertension, sickle cell and many more that I don't remember. There is so much treatment these days but each case is different. Most of the time the flooding that quite often happens in Africa brings a lot of suffering to the people. I have been lucky, as I always had the best treatment needed as well as my family.

I have always lived with Indian ideas. Whenever we have a gathering from birthdays, anniversaries, weddings, kids parties or barbecues, all the Asian community guys in the area tend to get together somewhere as the gentlemen love to wear just a simple outfit and maybe some gold jewellery; the ladies always look forward to an occasion so they can show off their new dresses, and how beautiful they look—from those lovely *punjabis* to the saris and the necklaces or the earrings; all enhance their natural beauty making them look graceful and attractive. They love to wear colourful dresses that have to be perfect.

Let's take an example from my family ladies; as they grew up they just had to buy that new style of sari, or get the chori (Indian blouse) tailored to perfection so everyone could really enjoy the combinations that had to be worn that special day. Woman love to wear *salwar kameez* and the *lehengas* called in Indian *ghagra cholis, churidar, gamchha, kurta, dupatta, sherwani,* to mention a few styles of clothing. The men like the traditional *dhoti, lungi* and the *kurta,* as the men love to wear shirts or T-shirts over mostly white *dhoti*. It's just amazing the way all the outfits look and the people themselves make this one spectacular experience every time. My dad loves the hats and the *jabas* (tops)—-it's just an unending variety.

CHAPTER FIFTEEN

• • •

I ALWAYS LOVED TO PLAY with the elephants! We used to go the rivers back in 1997, when I had the chance to play with them in real life. They love to be around water and eat a lot of vegetation; water keeps them cool and calm as they are quite intelligent animals. They go about in herds and can be in groups of 10 to 25 or more, depending on the area. An elephant is a big animal and I have sat on one of them while it walks––just an amazing experience!

Consider the giraffe, another of the animals I enjoyed watching. It has a long neck and walks sedately, eating leaves from the top of the trees. I really love the wild animals and it's always a pleasure to see one. The monkey has always been a companion to the African man. There are so many different animals out there––they make up a long list when you start looking around. Have you seen an antelope and maybe a cheetah? I think you just have to travel to Africa to experience it all in real life.

As we grew up my brother loved to travel to Vilaculos. It's in the same Inhambane district, but rather further from where we lived. He enjoyed the crystal clear waters of Dugong beach. I love the wildlife there as it includes some of the most exotic fish species. They have the most. They have the most luxurious looking lodges there. My brother loved the water skiing and windsurfing and deep sea fishing. We had to hire the boats available so we could explore the coral reefs and managed to see the vast range of fish species there are in the hidden treasures of the island; there are more than 300 different bird species, not forgetting the crab plover and mangrove kingfisher. You get fantastic views when you're diving. Dugong Beach Lodge is situated in the idyllic Vilanculos wildlife sanctuary and it covers 30,000 hectares of pristine marine and wildlife territory. The guests have a chance of staying in luxury chalets and villas overlooking the ocean. My brother loved the shallow water and the creatures that you get to see like the turtle, sailfish and manta ray, whereas I loved to see the pelican and flamingo birds. I believe there is not a better coral reef site in the area––I have certainly not seen any better in my life: there is an endless range of fishes and birds, and the blue water makes the setting spectacular.

One morning as I woke up I heard my Mum saying something in the kitchen, as I thought we had visitors that day. As I started walking towards the bathroom I realised she had some new girls working for her as she was running her kitchen as usual where she had to prepare all that food for the family. As I was walking to the bathroom I thought I would just say hello and as I was just about to say something my Mum realised I was up. I heard her say, "Hello son, are you up then? I've got your breakfast on the table ready with toasted bread and an omelette and tea, but if you need anything tell the girls so they will help, okay?" I replied, "Okay mom, I should be fine!" Just then I saw this nice looking girl wearing the most beautiful African dress. I realised it was the *kapulana*––these are widely worn dresses on the African continent, as the Mozambican women love to wear them in different patterns and different colours. In earlier days these dresses were called *ka polana*, which means 'place of chief polano', as they are famous around the country. As I came out to get dressed and then went to the table to have my breakfast, Suzanna––for that was the name of the serving maid––came across bringing the hot teapot and the basket full of fresh bread which she placed on the table. I couldn't help admiring the special costumes these people cover themselves with. I think it's a lovely style of clothing as they look different and special; it symbolizes woman of wealth in Africa, and it harbours some kind of message always in each individual design, as it speaks of a social or historical happening in the distant past of some family. Consequently the dresses are worn on special days. There are lots of different sayings by lots of different people that try to make the dress very special, as there are a lot of different ways people have for marketing the dresses––to different areas and regions. *Kapulanas* are worn for many social events and in a lot of different colours and used for diverse jobs. After serving the tea to me, Suzanne just said something like *kanimambo*––I think it means "Thank you sir", and off she went back to her duties.

I think when I was small we kept calling these dresses *foias* (colourful dresses) as well, but I don't remember clearly as it's been so many years ago. Life in these sub-tropical countries has a need for this type of clothing, as the weather is always hot and quite humid near the seaside. There is a contrast when I compare these dresses to the dresses that Indian women wear, as we have the traditional saris. My Mum had a wide selection of them from different areas of India, and the garments are always changing as there are so many meanings to the colours; a green sari for instance signifies vegetation and indicates youth and freshness and innocence; white saris signify peace and gratefulness, while gold-printed ones express the latest craze among young woman in India; maroon saris are trendy and loved by almost everybody as they have a rich bright look and make the ladies look so elegant and extra special. There are the magenta saris where the fabric is made from silk, and these are very popular. My mom, like most women in the Indian community, has a passion for saris. As the fashion is always changing, there is always the need to modernise designs and colours. Simple embroidery helps to make that difference to the look and the style and the texture as it just gives that extra feminine quality. *Kapulana* however is what the local Africans love to wear.

Chapter Sixteen

• • •

INDIAN PEOPLE always have had a tradition for centuries of arranged marriages. Mine was one of them. They are planned by family members with the permission of the parents. Most Indian people still believe that personal values and tastes and the background and the caste, age and height are very important factors to have a successful marriage, and with so many important factors to consider to make a successful marriage work, the help of family members is valued. There are so-called 'love marriages' as well, and mostly they happen in urban areas and the big cities and towns. Here a factor to bear in mind is that such a marriage may not have the benefit of the blessings of the family, even for the only reason that it might be against the elder's decision.

Our marriages are normally for life, made in good faith and with the belief that it will continue and stand firm through good times or bad times. Divorce is very frowned upon in

India and Indians living around the world. It's believed by both the girl's and the boy's family that they should be compatible for each other and have an education (it's mostly the boy who must be more educated than the girl); astrological signs should be compatible, the boy's financial future should be acceptable to the girl and the family, as well as his profession; some are fully vegetarian orientated, against any form of alcohol and smoking as well. Both partners should have the same beliefs; language should be the same but can differ if one person is from overseas; religion is very important because of family traditions. The 'candidate' must normally look okay (be presentable). Age and height are important factors as the girl should be shorter and younger, but most important are the values and personal expectations of each person.

When we get married Indian girls love to decorate their hands and arms and legs for the groom; it's called *mehndi* (which means tattoos)––a temporary form of skin decoration; in most Asian-Indian related cultures we see this, mostly in weddings and big festivals; designs are usually drawn on the palms and feet; the henna tattoo is mainly for brides and used on many occasions, like *diwali,* family get-togethers and engagements. They use paste, using a plastic cone as a brush to apply the paste to the skin, sometimes wrapped to try to create more intense colours on the skin, as the final look can be brown and it can last for weeks. These are all ways to create all those special looks for the occasions, in other words a nice Indian style of make-up. The girls do look stunning when it all finally comes together. Some people love the body painting that is used in lots of countries, while people in England prefer tattoos. Indian *mahendi* has been used for many, many years.

The religion of Induism *(Indu Darma)* believes that the marriage must be compatible so that on the auspicious day of their marriage both bride and groom can receive a blessing from the elders and God, so that the couple will flourish and follow the *dharma;* and as the acceptance of the marriage is agreed on the particular day they exchange fruits and cloths and more valuables and at a later stage it will be conducted in accordance with religious rites and rituals with invited guests in the society they live in; the girl is then given away in holy matrimony to the future husband to be. There are modern arranged marriages in contrast to classical ones. It's all about the family background or prosperity, and what education each partner has received and what expectations each has. The unique circumstances of each partner is considered too, in each individual situation in which they might be involved or pressured by their loved ones. Money makes a big difference, as you know. I remember my Dad talked about different types of marriages like *brahma, daiva, arsha, gandharva, prajapatya, asura, rakshasa* and *paishacha.* Indian weddings are no joke and typically you can have more than 500 people to thousands attending, depending what family you are from. It can obviously be very expensive and the costs are typically helped by parents and from the family if from a lower class. A live instrument band is played and most have *bharat* (bridegroom family) dancing to music before coming to the wedding venue. The wedding rituals are performed and lots of food served and it can last a week—like mine did! We call this *shadi* or *shubb vivaha.*

Once married, Indu women wear red vermilion called *sindoor,* with red *kunkuma* on her forehead, and a flower in her hair and coloured bangles. *Mangal* sutra is a hanging small necklace to symbolize being married. *Agni* (sacred fire) is complete in the presence of witnesses and family, mostly in law and tradition; the bride and groom should embrace to be properly married. Married life is an opportunity to grow from life partners to soul mates with a strong unity of beliefs.

There are modern Hindu weddings which are much shorter and conducted under a wedding *mandap,* a canopy traditionally with four pillars. An important element or component of the ceremony is the sacred fire *(agni)* that is witness to the ceremony. It's quite an old tradition but long before and maybe today back in India the palanquin made of wood and decorated with jewels is used as the bride comes to her husband's house called *doli.* The priests perform quite a big role to help as it's a long and exciting *vivah* (wedding).

CHAPTER SEVENTEEN

• • •

AS WE GO BACK IN TIME we discover Mozambique had its time of slavery. In 1752 it was colonized by the Portuguese and as it went on into the 1800's, slaves performed a major part of the economy, being sent out to work in sugar plantations. Slaves at the time were also sent to Reunion and Mauritius, and to Brazil as well, and for the same purpose. The Portuguese were in control until late 1975 when Mozambique became independent. It was a different world altogether but times have changed to our new era. We are the new generation and today's people, but as you travel anywhere in the country there are traces of all those bad times of slavery, and the habits or customs from those times still linger on for some people, though it's all much advanced in many ways.

As I was growing up I learnt that during the times of the Portuguese colony, during the slavery era in fact, my grandfather had travelled from India to Angoche, up north in Nampula and settled there, at first finding a job in a local shop and making a living and sending money back to India to grandma. This was before my dad got married and well before I was born, when my dad and my aunties were all very small and still studying in India. This is going back to the 1950's and 1960's when they used live on an island called Diu, near Gujarat, and I still have some of their early pictures, black and white ones (as the times have moved on we have colour pictures now). They used to live on the money granddad sent and they used to labour around the island helping some tailoring and some traditional local work to pay their way as they used to go to school and grandmother did all the housework.

Back in India we still love to drink the local cows' milk and have handmade bread and all the lovely sweets, as they do all that; my dad was called by granddad to Africa in the 1960's, and worked in his shop, as by then grandmother and all the aunties had moved there too. Life was different altogether, with new prospects for them; then granddad used to sell lots of tea out of the plantations, and all the other local vegetables, plants and so on. So they settled back there and made it home, as my dad by 1965 and the years following had to join the Portuguese military personnel, as they were recruiting; he become a sergeant and used to drive around the big army trucks. I still have his old and still nicely preserved pictures that bring back those old times, memories of how a person can change over time—for he used to be quite a smart looking fellow! His travels brought him to Inhambane. That's when he met my mom and they decided to settle there.

As all this was happening my granddad moved to Inhambane––by 1970, and soon after my parents got married. I was born in 1971, and my granddad died in 1972. My dad moved to work in Maxixe, the other side of Inhambane Bay to work in a busy local shop. We all moved there and lived there for a few years, until my dad saved enough money to start his own business back in Inhambane, by 1974/1975. I now had a brother and a sister, with a gap of one year between their ages. As we all started growing up together, life was fun though it presented different challenges to each of us––but then people have always had to find a different way of making a way ahead. My family had the chance of enjoying an African lifestyle and my parents did just that, by making an effort to have such a large family and really living life to the full. It was always a matter of making a living, and being in such a beautiful seaside town made this a pleasant experience.

As time went by all of us grew up, old enough to be working and helping in the shops we had. We prospered, and life was more than just school and sports; we had lots of friends and new fast-changing challenges and entertainments as the world always presented new singers and new Hollywood and Bollywood movies; we had a chance to learn about foreign ideas and new ways of life as we had the chance of reading the old cowboys western books, not forgetting the cartoon books; and so we learnt what we could at school and from books and films as time went by.

As the time changed I always wanted to try a new world––a new terrain or new locale. I am now settled here in England

and selling curry and rice for a living. It's a nice way of enjoying the Indian cuisine and a good way of making a living, for I love the traditional Indian food that I work with. Indian food has its diversities and I think it's the best food in the world; but then it all depends on whether you like it or not. As I was born and grew up in an Indian family, Indian food lives in my blood and for me a nice curry has always been the best way of enjoying the company of a loyal and devoted wife and partner––for it's one big problem if you don't know how to cook! I am quite a lazy individual when it comes to cooking, and why not if you can have someone cooking for you at home and at work! A bit of hard work nevertheless always pays with the right idea behind the scene, reinforced by that tough willingness I believe in!

As I grew up Reny, my sister, used to ask me if we could go with her and play with the monkeys in the local park, and that was certainly fun. I think they call them chimpanzees around here and in most of the African nations. They are so funny and so cute. Reny used to like holding their hands and would play with them for hours and hours on end, as we just let them sit on our shoulders and we used to feed them with bananas and whatever we had. It was lovely to be there and just enjoy their company, and they look like us somehow! They tend to be more with their mothers until they are much older; in fact, we always had the mother looking at us while feeding them. The little babies are cute. There were these big monkeys that we used to see then, like Bonobos and gorillas. They all have their differences and we loved to be around them. Reny was always running around those tortoises and we watched the squirrels and birds and

I think chimpanzees, that have long arms and prominent mouths and skin that is bare around the palms, face and feet and bodies covered with hair, mostly dark looking. They love to climb the trees and to sleep on the top of vegetation and they eat insects and nuts as well; but they are so lovely—— we just loved that afternoon and had so much fun! Reny would talk about it at dinner for an hour and for the rest of the times when we recalled those memorable days as we grew up; she now talks to her two sons and I am their Uncle Chris! How times do change!

When, during the school holidays, my mom used to take as to Maputo, the capital city of Mozambique to see her brothers, we loved the *quibon* ice-cream, and the *batata fritas* (fries) and the soft drinks, and all those lovely and delicious eatables that we loved and you cannot in a million years forget; we had a chance to travel to Inhaca Island that is in the Bay of Maputo, and we would sit on the boat, a quite large and white boat. The boat trips are famous and the white sandy beaches were wonderful to see from the sea. We went to see the museum, the marine museum; it's quite a nice experience and we saw the Inhaca lighthouse as we stayed in those lovely bungalows. My mom just loved those bungalows, as the palm trees offered that magic feel, the air being so nice and fresh and the beds out this world. We slept in the bunk beds, which added to the sense of adventure. We enjoyed the flow of those hot water showers after we used the swimming pool. The resort offered so much choice. Diving is popular there, while my uncle loved parasailing; other activities include fishing, water skiing, snorkelling—you name it! Just find something to do and enjoy yourself—we certainly did. The seafood while we were there was just fabulous; we had a barbeque and they played music and we sat there until late. It really was fun. There is nothing like living the reality——words cannot describe how much we loved every minute of that holiday time on Inhaca Island in the company of my uncle. It was the nicest day out ever.

We loved going fishing as the afternoon so spent was a relaxing time. After morning school, we headed to Marracuene and helped the local fishermen for fun, and used to catch a lot of different types of fish. It was lovely to see the variety that there was then, and afterwards we jumped into their boats and went sailing for hours. It's just another experience that most people would love and should have as the seas offer so much fun. They caught queen fish, mackerel, barracuda and sea pike, job fish, pompano, kingfish, wahoo, dorado, king mackerel; the variety was amazing. You just have so much choice and you can't resist the opportunity to try and catch something different. The different species seem to be unending. It's not surprising perhaps that fishing is a way of life in our Inhambane harbour.

While growing up we used to have school trips. We had a chance to travel up north to see the River Zambezi, as it is in Tete province, in north Mozambique; we had a chance to see the hydro-electric power station built to produce electricity that is distributed to the area as well as sent to South Africa. The Cahora Bassa dam is the largest dam in the area, and the most significant tourist attraction. It was built, also, to store water and control flooding. It presents a fantastic view and what a construction, a wonder to behold! We stayed in

Cahora Bassa's Tiger Fish Lodge, situated on a hillside. It offers pleasant accommodation 40 meters above the water level, and has all the facilities you would need. We used to wander around the side of the river to see the beautiful panorama that it offered and played in the water as well as running around for fun. It's just good day out.

CHAPTER EIGHTEEN

• • •

MY MUM'S COOKING is something I followed with keen interest as I grew up, as Indian cuisine offers a vast and complex array of ideas. My Mum loved to use those herbs and spices, and she loved to cook vegetables as most Indians are vegetarians. Fruit does have a considerable influence on the Indian ways of preparation, and the techniques differ in individual cases. She loved to cook rice, *chapati, dall, channa,* different varieties of *dall, toor dall, mung dall, urad dall, masoor dall,* and she often used different oils like peanut oil, mustard oil, coconut oil, sunflower oil, soybean oil, as there is a need for desi ghee (clarified butter); we love to use cumin, coriander, ginger, clove, *garam massala* (spicy mixes), chilli pepper, black mustard seed, turmeric, fenugreek, garlic, tejpata, mint, curry leaves, cardamom, saffron, nutmeg and essence of rose water. Fresh vegetables are used day by day as they are common to every household. There are so many types of cuisine we have that are influenced by our Indian cities like the Punjabi cooking, *rajestani* cooking, *sindhi* cuisine, *bhojpuri* cuisine and the *kashmiri* cuisine, *bihari* cooking, *gujuraty* and the *sindhi*––you name it! There are so many as the country is massive.

Indian people have always loved the tandoori chicken, *paratha, puri* and *bhatora, roti,* not forgetting lamb or goat meat which is widely loved; we love the samosa with different fillings like *keema* (minced lamb), minced chicken; the *paneer* is homemade cheese; *pakoras* are the best and *papardoms* we call *pakoras (bhujiyas),* and several types of pickles known as *achar, kachori.* Mum's favourite items when it came to cooking were the sweets like *gulab jaman, jalebi, singori, laddu, barfi, halwa, bal mithai, kulfi, falooda, khaja, ras malai, gulk* and so many other varieties. She provided the biggest list of choice I ever came across. I so love all these foods––I think they are amongst the best, and that my Mum was the best cook in the world. We have the best and most famous types of kebabs, a great variety of them too.

Indian influences are something that lives with us as the sanskrit that we know is like *artha, avatara, dharma, kama, kala, moksha, nirvana, kala, shanti,* as in English I think is religion, miracle, irony, resurrection, sin, secular, tragedy, guilt, heaven, hell, incarnation, absolution and more meanings; it all influences our daily lives and so on. The architecture, textiles, craftsmanship, wood care and other Indian ideas are part of our daily lives and have been around for many years. It's a very interesting world that I live in which brings many new horizons for life in the Indian way, with all its variety.

I do enjoy the Indian end and the beginning of the year. This means Diwali in our religion, and the rangoli are the different styles of design that our people use to decorate the floors of the houses and churches and wherever they get together. As the time of year changes and months go by, we have the Diwali and in the Diwali, we have these special designs of rangoli, a popular form of art among Indian woman as rangoli is painted in the front or back of the house, on the ground with colourful rice powder. Lots of flower and bird designs are created and, with other colourful material and stones, different ideas are created as it brings beauty to the surroundings and welcomes everybody during Diwali. People like to wear new clothes and children get lots of presents and the goddess Laksmi is believed to visit our homes during this festive period. The houses are well lit and decorated, bringing joy and happiness to all the people. All over India and the rest of the world Indians love to follow the tradition, as different colours and rice for the Indians are signs of prosperity.

CHAPTER NINETEEN

• • •

I LOVE MOZAMBIQUE so much but the security issues have always been a concern in the big cities, as unemployment has always been a big problem in African countries. Mozambique is changing but there are all these so-called gangs that just have to spoil the flavour of life, making life a misery for others. No matter how much the local government tries to stop it, robberies, mugging, rape, murder, often occur. This needn't be the case as women should not be alone on the beaches, as attacks have often been in tourist areas. Normal precautions should always be taken, but in general Mozambican people are so friendly and warm and the attacks are not a problem for most local people. Bribery does exist but one can come to terms with this by negotiating with the threatening person, who will let you go since you can offer something.

Money talks as everyone is so helpful, but business as usual is the order of the day as everyone has to make a living somehow. The roads are full of people always rushing about following their routine; cars and trucks are everywhere in a seeming confusion of traffic, especially in larger cities where you have the usual rush under the hot sun; people love to travel in large busses as they are so cheap and you end up paying fares that amount to next to nothing, as car travel is a luxury for most of the people; the rich have the best, as usual, but I have friends that do have big 4x4 vehicles such as Pajeros, which are very necessity in the sand and beaches and the tourists love travelling in them, as is the way in Africa. Travelling is often accompanied by the zuke music that we like to listen to in our cars. It's a challenge, but as you get there you feel the total difference, as we are used to luxury in the developed countries. These days the big towns do offer modern shopping centres and it's all becoming much more of the same pattern; as time changes the modernised buildings and their surroundings become more familiar. You notice these more and more every time you return to the country. The caju (local drink) made of the peel of the cashew nut is just a man's excuse to experience a spirit whenever he has the opportunity of stopping at the kiosks to get the taste buds going. Don't forget your sunglasses when you leave, as I always had to go back to retrieve mine––bad habit!

One day the phone rang in the sitting room. As I picked up the phone I heard my little sister Alka shouting, saying we had to get ready because there was this weekend when everyone was invited to go and see the crocodiles. She kept on: "*Vamos todos aprontar, rapido!! os nossos amigos venhem nos buscar e vamos ao arquipelago de bazaruto, a marracune, avisa ai o irmao chris, acorda o!!*"––meaning, "We are going to see the crocodiles in Bazaruoto so get ready quickly!" To quote her words: *"-epa! que bom, assim nao esquece as cameras de tirar fotos ta bem?"* ("..so nice, so don't forget to take the cameras to take some pictures while there!"); *-e um sonho ir a esta ilha de sonhos,* she kept on ("...a true dream come true, to head to an island like that); *"...vamos, vamos e nao esquece das toalhas!!"* ("...get ready and don't leave the towels behind!") We hastened to travel to the islands by road; she just was unstoppable as she kept saying: *"...esses crocodilos sao grandes nao mano?"* ("...those creatures are enormous, right?"); *"e eles sao tao perigosos quando com fome nao mano?"* ("They can be dangerous when hungry, right?") —–as we got to the island's surroundings and nearer the sea. The Bazaruto Archipelago compromises the Magaruque Island, Benguerra and Crocodile Bazaruto as well as the Santa Carolina Island *(Ilha de Paraiso–—Paradise Island).* It's got so much of fauna and flora and *o mato* (the forest), and wetland ecosystems and savannahs. She went on: *"...puxa isto aqui e tao bonito e cheio de mato!!"* ("It's so beautiful and full of vegetation!") It has wildlife beaches and turquoise waters, grassland scrub and wetland and thick forests, coconut palms; and cashew nut trees are on the shores. The freshwater lakes in the area are home to the famous crocodiles. *"...mano. vamos ver os coral reefs ai?"*—–"...let's check the coral reefs," she said. The coral reefs are sheer beauty as the tropical fish exist to make that nice view, for the archipelago is known as the 'The Pearl of the Indian ocean'.

"...olha irmao, os crocodilos sao tao grandes?" my sister said. ("...the crocodiles are so large?"), and added: "e tantos!!" ("Lots of them!"). As the day went by we had lunch and all went shopping while I decided to have a nap before heading to the water for a quick swim. I enjoyed the tropical hot feel of the water. It was quiet but I could still see a few people playing around in the late afternoon as the coast guards kept doing their routine job checking to see that people were not in trouble. We had to get back later that night——an enjoyable outing but at the end of the day it was home sweet home!

The next day here she was again up and shouting: *"-vamos, vamos!!"* ("...lets go, lets go!") I replied quickly as we hurried again to finish the weekend in Vilanculos: *"-sim menina, tamos a caminho"* ("...we are on the way, girl"). As we got to Vilanculos, we got into the boat that we hired for the day and ended up again checking out the crocodiles and a lot of other species the island offers. She was always saying something: *"-mano, viste os animais ali?"* ("Did you see the animals?") There are other animals like samango monkeys, different mammalian species, butterfly species and the birds——the varieties are enormous, we noticed, as we travelled by boat——a speedboat; she was always screaming with excitement as she pointed out something new: *"Mano, olha os peixes!!"* ("Brother, look at the fish!") The reef is home to a massive selection of fishes, like parrot fish, angel fish, puffer fish, wrasse, clown fish, octopus, bass, grouper, cod fish. The fresh water offers ideal conditions for the crocodile, red duiker, dolphin, dugong, game fish, samango monkey, marine turtle, not forgetting the giant lobster, sea horse, manta ray, shark, lion fish, and many more.

The number of bird species is quite massive too. Flamingos are the most eye-catching. As we decided to check out the wonders of the national park we saw the divers enjoying the scuba diving paradise in the crystal clear waters, and the dazzling soft coral reefs and ridges being explored. The most exciting reef fish are found there, such as snappers and surgeon, not forgetting the potato bass, barracudas, kingfish, reef sharks, manta rays, and the dolphins which are always around; the humpback whales can be seen sometimes in the year, as well as leatherback, loggerhead and green turtles, so beautiful to look at and there are so many other species which you will see as you travel in the islands.

"-olha os crocodilos e flamingos!!" I heard my sister again, meaning "Look at the crocodiles and flamingos bro!" I think my little sister loved the day so much––it was just so memorable. *"-aonde e que vais hoje?"* ("Where are you going today, man?") she asked pertinently. *"-vou a caminho da estrada para nacala ver o primo!"*––"I am going to see our cousin's brother up north," I answered. *"-ta bom, mas as estradas nao tao boas!!"*––"The national roads are not in good condition!" she replied.

In Mozambique we do not have very good roads, neither is the public transport network very good––but it's improving as time goes by. There are limited train services as they only operate from some big towns to neighbouring countries. The buses only operate from major towns where roads are in good condition, since in rural areas you may catch a ride in converted passenger trucks, *chapa cens,* or just *chapas,* or the normal trucks *(camions);* along the coast there are some ferry services but only in some major towns. Driving is not easy as there are lots of potholes due to the severe impact of floods, and there is a big need of 4x4s. There is lots of international help, however. Some parts are in better condition though potholes are the biggest hazard, and there are also the road blocks. Generally it's fine, once you get used to the general road conditions. I am used to all that as I lived there for many years.

Most of the shopping in the country occurs in the coastal shops, which are filled with tourists on account of the very unusual items that are for sale. Foreigners love to buy souvenir items there, as the large department stores are located in the bigger cities. Shopping in small towns is much more exciting as the street vendors *(domanemgue)* sell everything under the sun; these are located in the less frequented places. Shopping is becoming more popular as there is more international investment being made as incentives for growth, as the tourists love the art and craft world of ideas. The items made from wood are quite famous products; intricate cravings are created in wood and sold in the shops and streets, as lots of visitors take them back to wherever they come from. Examples of such items are the unique and different colourful masks that are on display everywhere; they are decorative displays on house walls, the material used being from local wood. Then there are the printed cloths, leather articles, baskets and pottery. Women or girls love to buy wire, malachite, soapstone and ornaments made out of wood. I often visited my dad's shop and the locals were always trying to sell these beautiful items, but how many can you buy? These articles are a nice way to remember your holiday while anywhere in the world.

CHAPTER TWENTY

• • •

LET'S LOOK AT THE FACTS. As far as I know, the country Mozambique is comparable to the size of Turkey, as it covers 801,590 square kilometres and is the 36th largest country in the world. It's two hours ahead of Greenwich mean time. It boasts a tropical climate with two seasons, a wet one in October to March and a dry one from April to September. The capital city is Maputo. Rainfall can be heavy but decreases North to South, and cyclones are present during the wet season. The best times to visit are in May to November when the lowest temperatures and rainfall occur. In February to April flooding is common and the roads are bad. The holiday season brings lots of visitors, especially over New Year, Easter and Christmas. Since new technology is available now, the internet and cell phones, it is easy to make bookings from across the world. The dialling code is +258 for international countries. It's not a dangerous place to visit but precautions are important for the individual. Drivers should give way to the right, drive on the left-hand side of the road, wear seatbelts, and observe the speed limit of 70 km/hour on open roads and 40km/hour in cities and towns; travel documents like drivers' licences are important and drivers should bear in mind the distances are massive: make sure you get enough petrol or diesel before setting out on your journey. I think the rest is just common sense, right?

My friend Joao, one of my school mates, invited me to his house as his mom was having a family gathering of some sort, and I had a chance to learn some traditional cooking that the locals love, like fresh stews, rice, corn porridge, fresh sea food, millet (a type of grain); cassava are as basic as the meat, chicken, steak, often accompanied with cassava, beans, chips, cashew nuts, coconut and potatoes, accompanied again by a variety of spices including garlic and peppers.

Puddings are made of fruit and rice, especially fruit like pineapple and papaya, and tea is an important beverage with which to finish the meal. Breakfasts consist of tea or coffee with mostly sandwiches made of egg or fresh fish, or a bread cake. Food stalls are everywhere and steak sandwiches are famous. Burgers, fried chicken, meat stews, and rice are often on the menu, and the restaurants always have fresh fish, prawns, calamari (squid), crab. Lobster and crayfish are often served with rice or fries. Matata is a peanut and seafood stew and a famous local dish. *Posho* is a kids' lunch (maize porridge). Toasted cheese sandwiches and chips are everyday favourites.

There are common ingredients for traditional African foods like the spices, pilau mix, curry powder, nutmeg, turmeric, cardamom, cloves, black peppercorns, garlic, melegueta pepper; lemon and rice are essential; meats are mostly chicken, pork, beef or fish of whatever is available; then, vegetables like groundnuts, sweet potatoes, corn, peas, cassava, watermelon, yams and okra. Mostly it's all cooked outside the house and on the traditional pots on the top of three stones and wood is used for fire and cooking. The traditional spicy cooking of Zambezi is famous as the chicken Zambezian style is grilled with palm oil and special spices. Joao, my friend, kept serving me with so much food! I still remember it all as the biggest *manjar* I ever had in his house; there couldn't have been more choice.

As I got on with life I found the diversity of Indian dances and Punjabi folk dances so special. Punjab for instance has very rich and diverse Punjabi folk dances. They are full of vocal remarks, gestures and are full of expressions. There are so many different kinds in the regions of Punjab in India; we used to see them dance *bangra* (the most popular), then *liddi, julli, jhumar, giddha, sammi, dhamal, dankara, jaago, teeyan, luddi, kikli* and *gatka*. They are all full of energy, vigorous and dynamic dances of the historic punjabis that live in some parts of Africa with emigrants. The way they dress is quite different in style.

I did have a good education; in Mozambique it's in three stages: primary education, secondary education and higher education. Lots of people still don't have a chance of a good education as the national public education system still needs improving; nevertheless there are educational initiatives being organised. I managed to stay in school until secondary school, and what I learnt has stood me in good stead today; it made quite a difference for me in this society and when we make a difference our education is our biggest weapon in today's world, as I believe life itself revolves around understanding what's happening around us.

As I recall, there are plenty of plantations around the country of Mozambique and sugar plantations are quite popular in the south. There is that green look of vegetation as you drive on the motorways and head from where we lived to the capital city, and it's nice to see the people working and trying to make a living out of them. Once we ended up in Xinavane sugar plantations; we met the people there and they let us try the long sticks of the sweet sugar cane––it was so nice to suck those sugary juices, as you have to chew the cane first before you can taste it. We call it in Portuguese *cana de acucar* (sugar cane). It's quite popular in the local markets and the local people love it and often buy it. We often used to enjoy those cuts of cane ourselves. It was such fun. Sugar does bring lots of revenue to the country and a lot of people depend on the plantations to make a living, but there are problems with floods sometimes. It's quite a competitive market, but there is lots of demand so the locals make the most of the products to be sold. There is an expanding number of sugar factories as better seasons do help to increase production.

I love to see the green sight of those sugar cane fields every time––the green swathes of tea plantations too! As I said before, at the time my granddad settled in the north in Zambezi, he lived in Gurue, which is home to the biggest tea plantations in the southern hemisphere. It is situated in an alpine climate and located at the base of the second highest mountain in Mozambique, 2419 meters above sea level. This alpine climate is the average climate above the tree line, as the air temperature gets colder as it rises and has proved to be best for tea plantations. My granddad loved the Gurue Zambezian tea from the Namuli Mountain with its stunning scenery. It's good to see large plantations as they present such lovely views.

CHAPTER TWENTY-ONE

• • •

COUNTRIES IN AFRICA are full of vibrant and colourful party events that range from religious gatherings to music festivals. Some are cultural as any harvest seasonal party or any excuse is all Africans need to celebrate the biggest festival imaginable! I recall the times I used to go to local parties in Inhambane, in the suburbs, as the places we used to go over the weekends were full of people wanting to have fun, with any excuse to have a beer or wine or just get drunk so they can relax and forget the heavy workload of the week before or the week ahead. Every time my mates and I just loved the atmosphere––the lovely lighting they had in the nightclubs, and the loud music when you got inside the building, or the so-called *casas de palhotas* (houses made out of wood and tree leaves). As we got in, the *guardas* (security personnel) always checked if we had paid for the tickets, and then we bought our *cervejas* (beer) and found a place to sit where we felt most comfortable. The lighting drew your attention, though not as much as the lovely girls who caught your eye with their attractive dresses worn for the occasions; then there was the impact of the loud music, and what a feeling! It got you in the mood to start dancing, just as the alcohol began making its impact on your system. Mostly everyone is quite friendly as you have to find your way, looking about to find a partner for that lovely *zuke* or *lambada* or any of today's latest album hits. The DJ's played the most vibrant of songs that were enjoyed far into the night. I have always loved dancing, and I have enjoyed myself in many of the memorable outings, as the weather is so hot it just makes you want to find your mates and get out––any excuse to go out and about in our quest for fun. We loved to feel the breeze in our faces as we danced through the night in those lovely discotheques (nightclubs).

The continent of Africa, especially Mozambique, is so rich in its culture as the family activities and the ethnic groups make a difference. The literature, music and art are the central activities; there are religious national dances and a lot of artists creating something new like new era songs and writers are all making a difference every time.

Africa was the birthplace of the human species millions of years ago, and most of the inhabitants are still indigenous in origin. There are a lot of diverse people and they do practice hundreds of distinct religions, live diverse ways of life and get engaged in a lot of different economic activities. Centuries ago different continental people settled in Mozambique like Europeans and Arabs and the Indians, like my family. There are lots of tribes in Africa like the Zulu, Senufo, Tuareg, Wolof, Yoruba, Afar, Anlo, Ewe, Ashanti, Amhara,

Bakongo, Bambara, Bemba, Bobo, Berber, Maasai, Ibos, Fulani, Fang, Fon, Kikuyu, Dogon, Chewa, Bushmen/San––quite a list that I still remember since my schooldays.

Is it true that whenever you want to have a good time you always find somewhere to go? As I love to go out I find that if you go to different places every time, even just to do your shopping, it's going to be a nice new experience, right? Every time I intend to change the way I buy my much-needed stuff, as I discovered that buying cheap goods always works for me just as well as buying expensive goods. Perhaps this is because I never had much money in the past, and this has reinforced the habit of living frugally? Is it me or is it the only way? Back in the land of Inhambane we believed that 'a saved penny is a help next time'! My pennies made a difference all the time since I didn't have much of a choice anyway, as life was always getting expensive. Weddings back in the land of Inhambane or the rest of the country were a big commitment and in the first instance involved two people in love; beyond that, two families were involved too, as a matter of course, which had a spiralling effect throughout the surrounding community because there is always an established network of people, mostly in the smaller towns and villages, who know one another. Apart from the knock-on expenses involved when it comes to inviting wedding guests, there is the wide range of different idealisms, as the traditions of the different communities can vary. As I said before, compatibility of the two persons marrying is something the whole community will consider, especially as the bride is the most respected person in the forthcoming marriage. It takes a lot of family training to know how to make the right decisions as the time arises, as there are many different requirements in a lot of different communities. The marital couple themselves must learn the secret codes and languages so they can communicate when married.

Traditional-event marriages involve dancing for days as feasting is important, and varies from the simple to the traditional, and sometimes there are lots of couples getting married on the same day where you get to see huge ceremonies. There are lots of gifts involved and clothing is most essential. I have witnessed lots of them as it's so much fun, and you really need to be present during the ceremony and celebrations so you can feel the real atmosphere. It's quite colourful, the way they dress and the food and drink style——it's just unique as it varies for each individual occasion. Dancing is mostly a very happy way for the people to show their happiness as it's so uniquely African——a special way of enjoying the occasion.

There are many memories going back in time and I will try to revive some by trying to say some of the sayings the people back there love: Inhambane, the land of lovely people, my little, loved town, it's so beautiful to see the sun set and sun rise, the lovely bay, and the sea with never-ending vista of water; there is this magic, the palm trees always looking stunning as you walk on the paved paths, the flowers always smiling at you and people always on their routine walks while the wind flows, the boats making their way on the bay; happiness is always evident in people's smiles. The unforgettable past lives with you in the present, episodes that you can never forget, the happy times that you cannot bring back as it is all right there, when you want to remember.

There are lots of different events happening everywhere as people commemorate certain festive occasions. I happened to travel to the Tofo festival that happens once annually and is held on Tofo Beach; a big crowd was gathering, the people enjoying the festive day under the sun.

Some time ago I managed to be present at the festival of the Zavala Marimbeiros in Zavala where everyone loves to play the timbila, and they are quite famous as well. We have had private events with lots of friends and relatives in these locations that exude a lot of luxury with lots of tourists who love the beaches where there are lots of villas, yachts and jets, not forgetting the deep blue water of the sea. These events often occur when there is a special occasion and I always had a chance to enjoy tasty food like grilled chicken and lots of other local specialities like samosas and *rissois* and *moelas assadas* with the local beer. There are also the occasional local shows as at the airport of Inhambane, where local bands attract a massive crowd to see them, like the *laka laka*. I welcome any excuse to get drunk as there are lots of special occasions to be enjoyed.

Chapter Twenty-Two

• • •

MY MIND often goes back to the time when my parents took me to India to see my granddad's house on an island called Diu. This was in 1977 when I was six or seven years old. We travelled by airplane and it was an experience you never forget––when you travel by air for the first time. We saw a lot of the country while travelling, as India is a massive place, the size of a continent, in fact. Travelling from east to west and north to south one encompasses so much variety, seeing different customs, people with different looks, and lots of languages, lots of deserts on the west to the snows in Himalayas, ranging from the dry heat of the central plateau to the cool forest foothills, as the land spreads through different lifestyles; lots of festive seasons are linked to big harvests of crops and cultivation and different religious festivals are an everyday occurrence.

It was then my dad said we should break our travels by stopping in Ahmedabad, to see the Bhadra Fort. After that we travelled to Lothal, about 87km, to see some ancient sites like the Indus valley civilisation excavations named Harappan. We then moved on to Palitana to see about 800 or so different temples with all the architectural styles. The most memorable of them all that I still remember is in Rajkot in Gujarat, a state in western India. The father of the nation, Mahatma Gandhi, received his education in Rajkot. One of the most historic cities of Gujarat is Junagarth. Then we ended up in Somnath to see the legendary shore temple, as the *Sasan Gir* was a nice time to see the animals like the tiger and big cats. We ended up in Diu where we stopped at home for our holiday, and it was altogether just a typical small Indian town.

We went to see the *gai* (cows) and the *rickshaws* (motor bikes driven by taxi drivers). All these ideally typical Indian towns offer quite different lifestyles; when get to understand the people you realise the differences are what you would expect to find, people always being so unique. It's just the way it should be, you feel, as you get used to them. It's always been as though 'life juggles around something', as the Bollywood song says; it's something that I have loved to listen to since childhood, like the rest of my family, especially melodies; there are many famous songs but I have a few favourites— the mother India songs, love story songs, *hum aapke hain koun, kaho naa pyar hai* songs and many more; it's such a variety and diversity of styles, all so fascinating and lovely to listen to.

In the early days when I was much smaller the all India radio was quite famous, and my aunties loved the way the radio station used to broadcast. I used to follow developments on the radio but then I moved on to the computer world where I get better access to whatever I am looking for, and much quicker, I guess. It's a rapidly challenging world we live in as the ideas I get to experience everywhere are different, especially when it comes to cooking and the presentation of meals. I think the best Indian *massala* is the *pav bhaji massala,* then the *pani puri masala; biriani massalss* are the best, for people love the diversity—*achar gost massala,* garlic pickle, *korma* curry *massala, kofta massala, nihari* curry *massala, karahi* fry paste, kabab massala, *kadhi massala, kesar falooda massala,* the favourite *chana massala,* not forgetting *chaat* and *garam* masala. These days there are more varieties, like madras rasan massala and so on. It is just amazing, the creations that there are these days. It's nice to try different foods! The challenging world of shopping is so diverse, and the online shops have everything available for you at your fingertips. I often have the chance to buy from these.

The Indian bookstores are something I like, as you move quickly on to Indian concert music, Indian jewellery, Indian musical instruments, yoga and health, which is something I like to check out sometimes. Indian dresses and the DVD stores also abound; sometimes with my niece we check out the Asian toys and games. It's a convenient way these days of shopping. I enjoy it.

Everyone loves the vegetables and fruits of India; my family always lived in a close relationship with fruit as we have a juice maker at our homes and most of my family members love the fresh juices as there is so much diversity, with anyone loving the juices with different recipes all the time, the older ones preferring juices with less sugar and the younger ones the recipes with extra sugar! But back in Inhambane Mercado central, where my dad still trades today, we have a vast selection of fruit like *uva* (grapes), *tangerine* (tangerine), *suco de laranja* (oranje juice), *pistache* (pistachio), *pera* (pear), *morango* (strawbury), *melao* (melon), *malancia* (like melon), *manga* (mango), *maca* (apple), kiwi, *mamao, laranja, jabuticaba, goiaba, figo* (apricot), *caqui,* banana, *ameixa, abacaxi, abacate* and many more available in season, and also so many more than are imported but tinned.

The older generation like my grandmother always loved vegetables like *tomate* (tamatoes), *suco de tomate* (tamato juice), *pepino* (cucumber), *pimentao* (green pepers), *cogumelo* (mushroom), *cebola* (onions), *berinjela* (eggplant aubergine), *repolho, rabanete, quiabo, palmito, nabo, maxixe, mandioca, jilo, legumes cuzidos, inhame cozido, folhas, couve-flor, cenoura* (carrot), *brocolis, beterraba, batata frita, batata* (potatoes*)*, *aspargo, alcachofra, abobrinha, abobora*––such a big variety but there are so many more as the family always loved new taste adventures, as there is no end to the way people love experimenting.

Traditional medicine has always been a part of our lives back in either Mozambique or India, where my ancestors learned a lot of medicine, as we now use it in our everyday lives. The use of medicinal plants is something ancient now––it lives with us today since the tradition goes back to the land that supported us. The use of plants for medicine is a big art that's been passed on over centuries, generation by generation, just as the indigenous population still passes it on to the next generations by practice. Today in my home we have all these ideas that we used in bygone days and learned from my grandmother. Many of these remedies still work better than today's expensive medicines. As one's health comes first, lots of plants are sold on the local markets, with lots of species, which can come from far away or they might have been grown locally; it's very important knowing all of this, knowing which plants are the most ideal for certain cures. There are lots of new ideas still being discovered by the researchers as time goes by. I learned about the ones from home and they are of great value and use to me. It's an interesting world—the traditional medicine that African people have learnt about and developed.

CHAPTER TWENTY-THREE

• • •

THE FRESH FOOD FESTIVAL in Mozambique is something I love and I often end up in one of them, as it's a different and fabulous feast of special cuisine in a veritable garden of delights what with the variety of music thrown in for good measure! The traditional flowers and farm markets are set up in attractive stalls––a big attraction, and the stalls offer the best of seasonal and regional produce; there are spicy chutneys and special sauces on sale as well, together with succulent meat and preserves. The Domaneghe market back in the suburbs of Inhambane presents demonstrations of culinary ideas in a special kitchen, as the traders bring a taste of a traditional country town trading into the heart of modern or crowded little stalls. The kitchens are set up to demonstrate different styles of food with local chefs showing their skills. At the same time everyone has a chance to learn a different range of useful and fascinating cookery hints and tips––good for the inspiration, as the experts do have the chance to advise anyone interested on cooking, planting, cultivating, not forgetting the harvesting of the local grown produce. I love these sorts of events, as you can try different stuff while your family or friends can have a nice day shopping as well. It's all great fun.

There are so many festivals in Indian culture and my family loves the *holi*––the festival of colours, as it's celebrated after full moon in early March every year. It's a day where everyone throws bright coloured powder and water at each other as young lovers cohort about in the streets and have fun, a tradition in accordance with the mythological expression of the immortal love of Krishna and Radha, going back to the early days way back in time. There are huge bonfires, and they are accompanied by folk songs and dances. The festival begins on the night of the full moon, as the bonfires are lit on the street corners to cleanse the air of evil spirits and bad vibes to symbolize the destruction of the wicked Holika, after whom the festival is named. People have a chance to drink *thandai* and *bhang* (these are marijuana based). There are different ways people enjoy the day as there is so much running, shouting, splashing and giggling. I got really coloured all over, several times, on this special festive day as friends put so much colour on your clothes and all over you––but it's fun, the only consequence being your clothes will end up looking very colourful, pretty looking and funny as well!

The annual festival of *raksha bandhan* is something that lives with me every year, as it means to commemorate the abiding ties between siblings of the opposite sex. The festival is normally held around August, and is marked by a simple ceremony in which a sister ties a *rakhi* (it can be a colourful thread, a decorative string or a bracelet) around her brother's wrist. The word *raksha* means 'protection' and *bandhan* means 'a relation of love and care'; it is followed by *aarti* (fire, this being a way to conduct a ceremony) when the siblings give each other their blessings in the form of sweets as a form of well wishing, and the brother gives a gift and some money as well. It's believed that the brother does express an extended protection to his sister as it's important to define the relationship. The festival is believed to enhance or strengthen the relationship, expressed by means of a sacred thread that symbolises the tightening of the mutual affections. I really enjoy the occasion as I have three sisters.

CHAPTER TWENTY-FOUR

• • •

WHILE ON HOLIDAY back in 1997 to get married, I travelled by plane from Heathrow to Johannesburg and then by luxury bus in an eight-hour journey to Maputo, stopping in Swaziland after a six-hour drive via Nelspruit for a break. I had a lovely lunch in one of those chicken burger restaurants, and I still remember how lovely it was; then the bus continued across the border to enter Mozambique after the passport check and the luggage inspection. I reckon that travelling in a bus is a long and tiring experience, but it has its own dimension of fun, for you get to see a lot of the mountains and roads and people travelling in their lovely cars and you see the lovely views of mother nature——as South Africa presents to view a lot of long and really lovely looking plantations, orange fields and sugar plantations and many more. You get a chance to see the very clean and beautiful never-ending roads and the lovely constructions: the way the houses have been built are just fantastic. When you cross the border and head to the capital city of Maputo, it's a different history that you witness altogether: while it may appear run down compared to other cities, it has its own charm: the picturesque station is one of many beautiful spots around the city where you can still feel the European influence. When I eventually got to the city the markets where bursting with lots of activity, as the traditional fish market sells seafood. I had to stop to soak up the real experience, to see those fishermen selling truckloads of prawns of every size. These markets are located in marginal areas (near the sea locations). The shrimps are my favourite. When I went to a restaurant called Costa del Sol to eat with my family, those fried king prawns with fried chips were delicious. The gin and tonic completed a lovely meal. Most of the people just like to eat these types of specialities. This repast was welcome since the next day it was back to travelling on a local bus, heading home to Inhambane City where my parents live. These local busses are full of crowded local people and can be taxing, at times exhausting because the distances to be covered are quite vast. Nevertheless, it's the best way available to get to see the entire panoramic world of Mozambique.

As I met Cuban people during the time of the civil war when I was little, back in 1995, I remember we used to participate in Cuban folk dances, what they call Afro-Cuban dances; there are many different styles but we loved to dance cha-cha-cha and mambo, amongst others I still remember, like rumba, son, casino (Cuban salsa), palo, danza and many more. As it manifests some Spanish influence as well as Mexican, these are loved in lots of countries. I frequently enjoyed these dances as we drank tequila with salt and lemon, an exotic experience as they come from a different culture altogether.

CHAPTER TWENTY-FIVE

. . .

I HAVE VIVID MEMORIES of staying at my granddad's house in Diu, in India. Diu is a small Island situated off the Saurashtra coast and it's connected to Gujarat. It's so small it's not surprising it only has a small population. It's so laid-back that it's often visited by tourists on vacation, being so calm and having such a relaxed lifestyle, far removed from the worries of daily life. Its crystal clear waters are quite famous as the beach is nice and full of sand and sunshine. It's mostly humid and the local people are all involved in lots of different daily activities. I used often to visit the fort that was built by the rulers back in time 400 years ago, and there are lots of old buildings like museums and churches and old houses that are still standing that evoke those old time memories of how it used to be then. The local people are so friendly and the food so enjoyable; I loved the cold drinks and ice-cream a lot because the weather there is normally quite hot all year round; for that reason you can do without shoes, and most of the time I only wore sandals. It's a small island full of fun and lots of people get married there.

While in India my dad took all the family to see the Taj Mahal in Agra. It is of course one of the seven wonders of the world, and is a symbol of love having been built by Shah Jahan in memory of his beloved wife Mumtaz Mahal. The Taj Mahal is the symbol of undying love and it was built on the banks of the river Yamuna in Agra where it looks picture perfect. The monument is made of white marble all around. It's also a symbol of tourism in India as it draws photographers, artists, painters, poets, sculptors and all kinds of people from around the world to see it. It's a lovely place and we had a memorable time there as the building itself was so marvellous to look at and admire.

Traveling is something I have been lucky with and lots of time I had a chance to travel to the second largest city in central Mozambique—Beira, the major port and railway junction, where the old Mediterranean-style buildings are still around. The *praca* (heart of the city) is the main square, where the old looking shops, markets and offices have their own unique style, where you get a chance to check out the cathedral and the *tchunga moyo* market. The city is full of imported goods and containers, and the old part of the port is full of wrecked vessels while the lighthouse forms part of a distant view. Beira city is lively and I have had so much fun shopping there, where the people always offer you their goods. It's quite a distance from the capital city Maputo, around 800 or more kilometres. It takes two days travelling to or from Maputo by bus and it's quite tiring.

I still relive the effects of the war back in time when I was much younger, as the civil war was quite brutal and conflicts where most destructive in Mozambique at the time. I think it lasted 16 years and a million or more people died through disease, violence and hunger. Lots more in millions were forced to flee from their homes, moving to neighbouring countries, so that schools and shops and hospitals were left in ruins. Civilians, especially woman and children, were the victims of the landmines, and casualties continued to happen long after the war was over. There were lots of mines still buried off main roads or the fields, so many people got wounded. It was not good at all and it still comes back to my memory again and again. Oxfam has been helping these poor souls ever since and it's a way forward to helping poverty and suffering.

Oxfam has played a big part in the rebuilding of the country. They helped to produce enough food for the hungry, and the farmers have their own ways of helping. The people are still illiterate but there is always a way of getting better deals somehow; there are some associations around, for instance, but progress is still very slow and income very limited. People get paid next to nothing, but are still very happy with their lives as it's such a lovely country and the natural resources are always there to help.

I have friends that love to work in the fields and are making a good living as the opportunities change with time. The schools are helping with the education, taking one big step at a time for the needy.

Life brings new horizons for you and me, and things do change at a rapid pace. I find it quite interesting, the way these changes all seem to revolve around you. I always look at life as most precious, and I have learned that it's all a big challenge and you have to keep fighting for a new tomorrow; but I believe that it's hard to compromise and at the same time make a way to a better future. How does a person relax? Do we have to be striving all the time, as though on the crest of a wave? I don't know, but something keeps me going!

There are some national songs and dance corporations today that I know that perform some of those artistic dances performed by women in Mozambique; these are a lot of traditional folklore dances that have been passed from generation to generation, as well as contemporary dances and a fusion of the two as well. There is a confidence of bringing forward a culture to today's people with the traditional *makway* and *ngoma* dances. *Makway* is a dance of joy and *ngoma* was a way to get the warriors ready for battle. The *niquetxe* dance expresses the frustration of the people that were forced at tea plantations to work with hard labour by the foreigners, and the *nondje* dance (giant tree) came originally from the north at times of war. These dancing habits are a reminder of the past for today's people, with lots of poetry being part of the practice as well. There are shows that frequently perform these dances.

I have lived my life enjoying myself somehow and nightlife for me has always been important, so whenever I could I always ended up in a nightclub where everything is so colourful and vibrant with lots of people out and about partying and dancing the night away. On one occasion we ended up in Feira Popular in the city of Maputo where we had a choice of going into bars, discos or clubs where I loved the local dances. Mini golf, too, was an attraction and used to be the best in my time in Maputo. Club 7 is remarkable but there are so many, and usually I ended up in the same place. The crowd was always good and the drinks so cheap; the lighting and the songs were just the best––I think you would love it all. The *Tamil Nadu* served there is excellent. I like it because it is based on spices and condiments and most of the dishes are cooked with coconut and tamarind. It's all mostly vegetarian recipes, such as the *garam massala* which is not used in *Tamilian* food; coconut oil is normally in the cooking. Everyone loves the chutneys and mixed spices and it's used for lunches in *tiffins,* where a typical meal consists of rice, lentils, grain and vegetables. There are some varieties with hot and spicy dishes like mutton, chicken and fish dishes. The famous dishes that I love when I am in one of those restaurants are *sambar, idli, massala dosa, massala vada, medu vada, pal payasam,* coconut chutney, *mulaga podi, ven pongal, chettinad* chicken, vegetable *uppama* and many more that are available like juices and fallodas and lots more.

I loved to go to beaches, often with friends, and the ocean has so many different creatures. I often used to come across jellyfish; we had to be quite careful as they seem to be such beautiful creatures but quite deadly. I love to see them floating under the blue water; they are delicate creatures and complex, and are made of 95% water and grow a lot; there are so many types of them out there. I just love looking at them swimming in the sea.

As I have travelled a lot around Africa I have learned a lot. Africa is a continent of extremes where you can find a lot of natural resources. I think it's the second largest continent on earth and it's an exhilarating place to live with that exotic feel in the air. There are lots of deserts like the Sahara. The tallest mountain is Kilimanjaro. It has a high population with rapid growth, millions of people living in urbanised areas. I have had a chance to visit some of the largest countries, like the Sudan and Egypt. Cairo is really crowded. I had the chance to see the Nile River, the longest river in the world. The Sahara desert is the largest desert in the world. There are lots of oil reserves, diamonds and gold, and there are so many lakes, Lake Victoria being the largest. Olduvai Gorge below Lake Victoria is considered to be where mankind had his origins. Africa has 53 independent countries each with its own complement of native people, cultures, economies and history. Africa has vast deserts, tropical rain forests, lots of fertile grasslands and tall mountains, lots of lakes and rivers, wild life reserves, lots of natural wealth; but there have been many famines and diseases that have afflicted the less educated people; nevertheless it is a beautiful land where hot weather is normal. You will only know the true extent and nature of Africa if you travel and see the reality for yourself.

I loved to go to the special dinners as the Mozambican dinners are unique and out of this world. The silverware, china and wine glasses are placed on the table in a decorative manner; the napkins and tablecloth are always used when the table is set. The cocktail bar as mostly stocked with scotch, soda water and ice and bottles of port, not forgetting the unique Portuguese touch of olives, where there is a choice of black or green. Usually there is a white table wine, chilled, as an aperitif. Soup might be offered as a starter as well as *matata,* an unusual peanut entree with white rice and piri piri with lots of salad. Dessert might be a choice of fruit. To finish the meal off coffee or tea is important; and then there are the liqueurs *(agua ardente).* The occasion might end with *fado* singing or some traditional songs and dances.

CHAPTER TWENTY-SIX

• • •

LIKE MANY INDIAN PEOPLE in this big world, I was born into an Indian family that believes in Hinduism. 70% or more Hindus are Vaishnavites, and we worship Lord Vishnu. There are various differences in Hinduism, like Hare Krishna and Sikhism. Most Indu people have their foreheads marked with coloured dots, like Bindi, Kumkum, Bottu, Tilaka or Bindiya. It's a sign of piety and lets people know that the wearer is Hindu.

Many women nowadays wear different colours on their foreheads to match their saris, while the men dress up mostly for important occasions. India is a land full of different and diverse festivals—I would say a land of festivals and these are presented all over the Indian country and the rest of the world. Indeed, there are many festivals and the Indian community is far-flung throughout the world.

Talking about Hinduism, we have the biggest belief in god and therefore we have temples all around the world, but especially a lot in India. Hindu temples were not meant for large congregational worship. Pillared *mandapas* with sculptures, sadas for dancing and wide passages constitute a temple complex. There are so many designs like the north Indian temples and southern Indian temples; there are many different styles in different areas. It's all an exciting and wonderful world that manifests the Indian way of showing respect for god.

Every time I travel to India I find that the climate is different around the year. It rains on a specific time of the year; there are often monsoons in the southwest and northeast. There are three seasons a year like summer, the rainy season and winter, and it can be very hot in the north and cold in the winter. April and May are quite rainy. The ancients had identified six seasons *(ritus): vasanta* (spring), *greeshma* (summer*), varsha* (rainy), *sharat* (autumn), *shishira* (winter), *hemanta* (mild-winter) They had the year divided into these sections.

My young sister Alka lives in Xai Xai and she is married with two little daughters. I often have a chance to travel to see them and enjoy a break. It's in Gaza province, near the river, and we love to go there quite often for fun, to see the water flowing downstream; we enjoyed the chance to feel the breeze on our faces while walking along. The kids just love to talk away: *"-olha a agua tio!"*—"Check out the water, Uncle!" shouted one of the kids. *"-e tao bonito de ver a agua nao e?"* ("It's so nice to see the water, right?") *"-isto aqui e so maravilhoso nao e?"* ("This river is so marvellous and lovely!!") they kept shouting.

As we went along I noticed that the Limpopo River, where the year 2000 floods took place, was so lovely; we had the chance of seeing the bridge that crosses over. It's just a little town built on the way to the capital city, close to the Indian ocean, about 200 kilometres from the capital, and where lots of people grow rice in the fertile soil. There are few little towns or small villages, like Tavene, Chiluane, Macandane and Dong Uene, which are old locations. Xai-Xai is very nice and my sister seemed to know everyone because they have a shop. There are restaurants, a post office, petrol stations, bars, a few furniture factories, and we love to go to the night club Miau Miau. It's so famous there. I often travelled to Resaano Garcia borders with my brother-in-law. He took me as well to Namaacha and Manjacaze. It's a tourist area as well because of the beaches, and the coral reef which is nearby, just a few kilometres away. There are some beach resorts too. You could call it 'the land of smiles', being a tropical holiday destination with its beautiful coastline, and being the friendliest of places where the people are very laid back. I have always had so much fun there!

My sister cooks good local food and I enjoyed the goat meat with beer and some vegetables; she does this mostly on Sundays because the shop is normally closed then. We went to the beach to have a picnic on the Praia de Xai-xai. The water is so blue there—there are no words to express it. My nieces love to see me so they can go out again for more fun, and why not?

There are so many dishes that I love to eat in the Mozambican way, and they are quite nice as I have tried a lot of them. My favourites are *matapa* (made with peanuts and *mandioca* leaves), *caril de galinha* (chicken curry), *caril de caranghejo* (crab curry), *caril de camarao com ananas* (prawn and pineapple *curry), caril de amendoim* (peanut curry); there are so many dishes I love, like *camaroes fritos* (fried prawns), *camarao com alho* (prawns with garlic), *camarao tigre grelhado* (tiger prawns grilled), *caldeirada de cabrito* (goat soup type), *ameijoas com leite de coco* (mussels with coconut milk), *arroz de bacalhau* (rice cooked with cod fish), *arroz de coco e papaya* (rice with coconut and papaya fruit), *bifinhos com caju* (meat cooked with cashew nut), *bolo catembe* (catembe cake), *bolo de caju e batata* (cashew nut cake and potatoes), *bolo de figo* and *mandioca* (mandioca cake).

My parents travelled from India in the early days and, like me, they found that country fascinating, with its many religions and communities that live together in unity. Indian people live there, of course, though the population is polygenetic; there is an amazing concentration of various races and cultures and it's impossible to find out the origin of the people, though there is different species known as *ramapithecus,* found in the Siwalik foothills of the north western Himalayas and believed to be the first in the line of hominids (human family) that lived some 14 million years ago; the *austrapithecus* lived in India some two million years ago as well and there are so many ethnic groups in India, like Nordic Aryans, mongoloids, Negrito, proto-austerity. In fact, India is the largest democracy, the seventh largest country, the population over one billion and the second most populated in the world. The capital city is New Delhi. It's quite industrial and produces a lot of steel and iron and it is mainly agricultural and it's close to the world's highest mountain chain. It's a fact that India is the largest democracy, and, as I said before, the seventh largest country, the population being over one billion and the second most populated country in the world.

In my house we speak different languages altogether and Guajarati is where my ancestors come from in India. As is known, Hindi is the most spoken language in India. Amongst Indian people 69% speak Indo-Aryan and 26% speak the Dravidian language, and 5% speak Tibeto-Burman. Lots of people use dialects and in the south of India many people speak Kannada, Tamil, Malayalam and Telugu; as my parents told me, in the north is spoken Bengali, Punjabi, Marathi and Guajarati, same as us.

Sanskrit and Tamil seem to be the classical languages as they are 3000 years old. While I was growing up my dad always spoke to me about his proud country and as I kept growing he insisted that I should learn how to read and write Guajarati. I had a chance to learn about a lot of Indian states and union territories, but especially he loves Diu, Daman and Goa, as they were Portuguese colony territories. There are a lot of them, like Kerala, Karnataka, Madhya Pradesh, Jharkhand, Jammu and Kashmir, Gujarat, Himachal Pradesh, Haryana, Goa, Bihar, Chhattisgarh, Assam, Bihar, Andra Pradesh, Arunachal Pradesh, West Bengal, Maharashtra, Manipur, Meghalaya, Mizoram, Orissa, Nagaland, Rajasthan, Punjab, Sikkim, Tamil Nadu, Tripura, Uttar Pradesh and Uttarakhand. The union territories are Puducherry, Daman and Diu, the national capital territory of Delhi, Lakshadweep, Chandigarh and Andaman and

Nicobar Islands. The largest cities that my dad has been to in India are Ahmadabad, Hyderabad, Bangalore, Chennai, Delhi, Kolkata and Mumbai.

Religion is something that lives in my everyday life, and my entire family talks about epic poems written from 500-100 BC, the Ramayana and Mahabharata during the puranic and epic periods; there are so many religions that we talk about a lot, like Jainism, Buddhism, Sikhism, Christianity, Islam and Hinduism. There are more but I am not aware of them. The Indian country is so massive in population as well; it's in billions and still growing.

The way we say hello may well give the impression of bowing and obeisance, but the style of salutation is meant to express respect; we say *namaste* or *namaskar,* maybe *namaskara* or *namaskaram* or sat *shri akal.* The most used is *namaskar,* being the most formal and expresses deep respect. People say *Salam* in most places. As is widely known, Hindu people like us don't really eat cow meat as it's regarded as a symbol of *ahimsa* (non-violence) and we are taught to respect the cow as a mother goddess, revered for bringing wealth and fortune; therefore respecting and feeding a cow is an act of worship.

Festive seasons are never ending in Indian culture as it's a multi-cultural and multi-religious society; there are three national holidays like *Gandhi Jayanti,* republic day and independence day, and the most popular I love is *dussehra, rakshabandhan, holi, durga puja, ganesh chaturthi* and *navratri* and the end-of-year *Diwali.* The harvest festivals are common like *onam, pongal* and *sankranthi.*

Islamic festivals are eid al-adha, eid ul-fitr *and* ramadan.

I find it all fascinating and it's an opportunity for me to have lots of sweets that I love so much!

Many times I have travelled to Bombay in India and, as everyone knows, it's one of the most crowded places in the world where millions of people live and work. Many times I have enjoyed the stay in the city, having gone there also to have my wife's operation done. I really enjoyed the rickshaws and the trains, not forgetting the lifestyle of the people rushing to and from work every day. I became one of them because, being of Indian origin, it is just a matter of speaking the language to blend in! It becomes so easy to get by. I loved the shopping and the pushing and shoving on and off the crowded trains during the rush hour, and being part of the thronging masses of people everywhere! There is a saying about this massive city like 'Bombay is happiness!'––where 'happiness' can be interchanged with words like longing, life, love, agony, opportunity, lust, loneliness, crowds, ecstasy, people, gods, demons, poverty, greed, affluence, power, frustration, privacy, space, fun, joy, strength, money, wealth... life never stops there: it's always noisy and it's a very dusty city, but there is always something happening. One famous saying goes, 'If you are tired of Bombay, you are tired of life!'

One thing I enjoyed while on holiday in Bombay is the beer bars where you get the chance to see Bollywood-type dances that attract many men in bars around the town for a fun night; the beer bars constitute a way of life in the enormous city. I had a chance to drink Kingfisher local beer and eat the peanuts and cashew nuts plus crisps, and a little salad made of chopped cucumber and chopped tomatoes while the girls were serving. The girls are so friendly and normally talk you into dancing with them and drinking more, and making you feel welcomed so all you want to do is stay and relax and drink and dance away and keep being entertained. The warm welcome and the pleasant Indian music are conducive to an atmosphere that encourages you to drink away and throw money at the serving girls in piles of 10 rupees! It is difficult to resist having a dance with them and enjoying their company until late, as they are so beautiful in the Indian dresses they wear for the occasion; they look so beautiful in their colourful dresses and saris, the traditional costume of the Panjabi's as well; there are so many different girls always changing partners––it's all so much fun it keeps you interested in dancing and drinking more, and the night soon flies away.

It is alleged that these girls act as a front for prostitution, but the beer bars are not illegal; they are a thriving industry which brings together bar owners, hoteliers and travellers. The dancing barmaids are hired to dance for the bars' clients so that the customers are kept entertained and spend more money and enjoy themselves. The clients are generally working class males, employees of high-class business executives, as well as visiting so-called tourists like me looking for fun and perhaps a bit of love (which they find if they are lucky)! It's a way of life that drives a lot of bread and butter into this city, and which also generates a lot of fun. Mostly, as it's quite normal, girls love to wear dresses of pink;

indeed, I find that Indian girls have a passion for pink saris; it's an attractive colour, and mostly everyone looks exquisite in this special costume. Often the dress is accompanied by some flowers, usually attached to the dress. The ready-made sari set consists of a blouse, petticoat and sari. The sari is attached to the petticoat and pleats are pre-made. The Palu can be worn the way you want, and it's always worn on important occasions like marriages and big functions and gatherings. It's India's most traditional dress.

One thing I always enjoyed in Bombay is the Indian snack known as *chevdo* (Bombay mix) or in east India *chanachur* (mostly fried lentils), which originate in the city of Mumbai and consists of a variable mixture of spicy dried ingredients like lentils, corn, peanuts, chickpeas, flour noodles, vegetable oil, flaked rice, fried onions and curry leaves––all flavoured with salt and spices with coriander and mustard seeds. I normally have them at restaurants and bars while out and about. It's a fun type of food and very light.

There are other very popular types of mixers specialities like *bhelpuri* and *makka poha,* not forgetting *sev mamra.* *Bhelpuri* is a puffed rice dish with tamarind sauce and small potatoes and lots of people enjoy it with onions, tomatoes and chillies. It gives a really nice taste in your mouth. *Sev mamra* is a mostly Indian typical snack with savoury noodles and rice with peanuts. *Makka poha* or *makai poha* is another snack usually made of corn or maize flakes and is fried on hot oil and served, as they say, like a nice mix called *farsan* (savoury), meaning *chevda* (a mix of all these spices). Ghugni is an evening snack usually in eastern India; *kala chana* (black gram), or dried peas cooked with gravy can be served with *kurmura* (puffed rice), or as well with *bhajia* (onion *pakora,* quite hot most of times). There are so many ideas out there and I love mostly *massala* tea with them.

How exciting it is when you come across two or three chillies! They can be fiery with that hotness to it when you chew them; the red or green chillies are part of everyday life for a typical Indian man or woman. Then the chutneys and cold drinks and juices are part of that large city of Bombay. I used to wander along Marine Drive and loved the salted roasted peanuts from Jehu beach; also chow patty, as there is plenty of other good stuff around the crowded beaches.

A drive through the old Mumbai can be quite exciting where there is plenty to discover; it is like being at the gateway of India where you get a chance to try grilled sandwiches, rolls, pizzas, and as you move on to Marine Drive you will see a lot of the tandoori kebabs and the world-famous dishes cooked in style, the tikkas, for instance. I love the Arabian Tent which offers *sharwarma* in various ways and in convenient picnic boxes, party boxes and family boxes, with many more choices. When I was in Chowpathy I loved the famous *bhel puris,* steaming *bhaturas, tikkis vadaas* and *paav bhajis* where *aji ali* were apart from vegetables like *paneer* sandwiches and other ideas like cauliflower or mushroom; you get the fresh fruit and fresh juices as well as fruit creams and milkshakes.

One more speciality is *schezwan* pizza and cheese grilled sandwiches as the *faloodas* are complemented by a nice refreshment milkshake type speciality, of which there is so much variety. As life changes, sex can be a hot topic around a few friends and as a man I love a bit of fun; while in holiday I loved to enjoy going into the beer bars where I had a chance to see and feel the real live shows, where many people make a living by entertaining the guests in town; as it is an intense desire of men to attract the girls, the attention the girls give them in the beer bars fulfils their need, enabling them to have a laugh and a bit of fun; it all operates through serious amounts of cash, the dancers giving pleasure to the man by touching and playing around, and keeping him company, which includes smoking and sharing a drink. At the bar everybody tries to smile and give you the best possible time. These bars do tend to flourish quite well, because customers are given that momentary feeling of joy and momentous power. Money does buy a bit of happiness but sex is something that is a reality and the girls do make a good income; the so-called customers like me go there just for fun, and I love the atmosphere with the old or new dances with loud music, the singers singing and the dancers dancing, people enjoying the smoky bar and the dance floor and the doorman always politely saluting people coming and going through the door. There is a chance of people catching some kind of illness but it's pure luck, and I believe life can be fun. When I come out of a club I generally get hungry; so after I went drinking in these beer bars I ended up buying myself an Indian pizza, which is really delicious and a pleasure to eat; it is bread spiced with cheese, massala powder, onions and lots of peppers. There so many names for these pizzas, like fusion pizzas. I think Bombay style pizzas are the best!

CHAPTER TWENTY-SEVEN

. . .

A NEW DAY brings a new adventure, and since wildlife is something that always lives on in me, I am always ready to take the opportunity of enjoying the wildlife while in India. I had a chance of seeing the Asian elephants and when I compare them to the African ones, they are bit smaller as their ear sizes are small; they are also easier to tame and have been used as beasts of burden for centuries in Indian territories. They can run up to 40 km per hour or more. These mammals are the largest creatures on earth, and in Asian culture they have been domesticated and used for transportation and are capable of moving heavy objects. Their skin looks brown and dark grey and they mostly live in herds. They make sounds like loud trumpeting and I like the way they eat grass, roots, bark and leaves and bananas, and they love to drink water all the time and consume lots of food. I love going to the big parks to check them out and watch them for hours.

Speaking of wildlife, the white Bengal tiger is one of my favourite animals and they are also called Indian tigers. There are many of them in and around India. They like water and they run up to 50 kilometres per hour and I like watching them while trying to make a kill. They sleep quite a lot, like 15 or more hours a day, and they roar loudly. The beautiful stripes help to camouflage them in grass and I like to see their jaws, so strong, that enable them to catch their prey. I think their strong sense of smell is a big help to them as well. They also swim swiftly in water, as I have witnessed many times during safaris throughout India.

Like other animals, the camel is one I have sat on a few times, and their long curved neck, deep narrow chest and the single hump, make them look quite comical. It's fun riding them but be sure to take something soft to sit on for while they move it can get uncomfortable! These herbivores eat dry grass and mostly thorny plants and they have I think a long relationship with humans as they provide meat, milk, leather, wool and help with transportation. It's fun riding them on the beach. I am enthralled by the size of their eyes, and their tongues are absolutely huge when you see them coming out of their big heads!

Being positive or maintaining a positive perspective or state of mind is something that lives on in me and I need a reminder that life is a challenge. I believe in goodness, kindness, laughter, having a big smile, love, appreciating the joy of the moment and a sunrise that makes me feel good. When I go to the beach any chair is a help to sit and relax and check out what is happening around me, and see that faraway blue water, that big sea that really makes me feel positive. It's fun having a book to read, maybe a beer and a mobile if you miss someone you like or love; you never know when anyone needs you. It's quite a nice way to feel renewed and to recharge your batteries for more fun and challenges that life may bring.

CHAPTER TWENTY-EIGHT

• • •

ENJOYING MYSELF has never been in doubt. I always make the most of any situation or challenge, but I don't tell everyone all my secrets; nevertheless I can tell you that while I was on a short break from work back in 1993, I really was tired mentally and I decided I needed a relaxing time away from the rat race lifestyle. Consequently I left the gates of Heathrow airport and its stunning carpets to go home and see the unpainted walls of my hometown and the really exciting old style of architecture that had been left by the Portuguese before I was born, a long time ago, even centuries ago. The drinks companies and the mobile phone companies have taken over the hoardings of most sites of the town that my parents live in, and I think after all, no matter, it looks good and different for the locals to have the best of the modern world of necessity and progress.

When I got home I was surprised to see that my mum really missed me but, after all, every mom would miss her child!

I was treated like a king and fed the best of food, cooked in the way she used to cook when I was small, which I really liked. The variety of food that she had on her menu was quite amazing. I had forgotten it all while I was away. After a week it ceased to be a novelty and everyone had gone back to their work and routine lifestyle––but then I met this gorgeous lady that would make my world so exciting, a lady called Sandra. It turned out to be the most memorable love encounter I ever had! It was just as though I was on a different level of airwaves whenever I was with her. I just could not stay away and just somehow wanted to be with her all the time; it was very unlike me––maybe it was just the time in life that I was looking for a companion and it happened by chance that she turned up at this moment––the right place and time! I got so involved with her and it was so much fun (all the time!), doing everything together, especially when riding a motorbike with her hands around my waist! It was just out of this world as I felt her breasts pressing on my back and the warmth of her body, talking silly things; just being with her was like being on another planet! One day we ended up on the local beach of Inhambane––Mabalane. I looked at her and there she was with this elegant body of hers with the most stunning bikini costume––wow! I just kept looking and... what would you do in my place? We ended up in the cold water and the leaves floating around us were something to play with. An old boat that was left there from the early days reminded me of the era of the pirates––maybe Captain Hook! We jumped into it and started playing, our arms beating the water like water-wheels as we pretended we were cruising away into the deep sea. After all the play and swimming, after getting tired, there she was on the floor of the boat, lying stretched out and looking at me. I just had to hold her and you know what happened? Have you ever made love in an old broken boat? It was just unbelievable––but then it happened so spontaneously, and I still remember it again and again. She was the girl of my dreams. To cap it all the feelings were mutual, and I really by then had forgotten the real world. Why? Because at that time, being at home, I was not paying any bills whatsoever––who would if you were staying with your parents? And here I was going to the functions and parties of friends around the town, and the best restaurants, because I was rich and single––no mortgage, no bills and wife. I really had the time of my life.

It was then one night that we went to the Tio Jamu bar and nightclub and somehow got in without paying. We sat at a table and ordered the beer and some samosas and *rissois* to eat, and when the music was on it turned to out to be the zuke night and what fun we had! We all danced, couples holding each other as we moved around the dance floor. As the night went on we really enjoyed ourselves. It was lovely listening to the music and letting the lighting get to you. We enjoyed the songs and the company of the friends and people around us; it was so much fun––it was a lovely time that I like to recall to memory in order to experience over and over again!

The relationship that I had with Sandra was just over a period of 3 to 4 months, at the time of my holiday back in 1993. She was a lovely girl, but born into a Christian family and of African descent. She had lovely parents and beautiful sisters and it was fun being around them at their house. I loved going there––it was really so nice meeting really friendly African family people. The young ones were so friendly, we used to chat away and play away in a garden, and it was a very different atmosphere altogether, having a chance to live an African family lifestyle. I was able to share their likes and dislikes, their food and enjoy the way everyone was kind, getting together and living together. They believed in their religion and education and did their best to adjust to the difficulties of the times, coming to terms with those remaining unforgettable years of the civil war, when the military personnel were always passing by while we sat on the pavements outside the house and talked about silly things and laughed about anything and everything; in spite of those difficult times we really enjoyed ourselves as much as we could.

Sandra had her own lifestyle and the way she was, was so different to what I was used to, and maybe I just loved to be with her at the time. We kind of loved riding the motorbike around the town, just feeling the breeze and going down to the seaside and playing around in the sand for hours and hours, holding hands and just walking, talking, chilling out––and there was this lovely feeling that I just can't describe––would you call it love in the air? Ha ha ha––nice, isn't it? It was just so special!

Camping is another way of enjoying a gathering and picnic and maybe a way to relax and enjoy a friend's company. I love doing this occasionally, but the weather is an important factor––it can get cold and chilly but it's worth doing because it has such a positive effect on my soul. Eating outside, al fresco is so lovely, and I don't know anyone that does not like to do so, as outdoors is so different and offers the chance to see new faces and really relax while you munch some food like a burger and a beer and feel alive. Outside, camping fires are nice at night; I like sitting near the fire and watching it, keeping warm; on cold nights it engenders a secure and cosy feeling, and you really know you are alive and well, and most of all really makes you enjoy a nice night's sleep.

A morning coffee in the sun is something really nice to remind you that life is still going on and maybe remind you to pray to God in thankfulness for the sun——or become a sun worshipper! It makes you appreciate the sun as life would be so boring without light and sunrays. Walking is something positive, too, a means of recharging yourself. It makes me feel good inside and I normally feel that good exercise is a way to engender positive thinking and see through, clearly, to what you want out of life. Time off work is a real way of enjoying yourself, but be sure to use the time effectively, for you need to relax and recharge your batteries after working, generally by chilling out, which is what I enjoy.

CHAPTER TWENTY-NINE

...

MY PARENTS have been or are the best, as they have always made sure that their children have had as much attention as possible; this applies especially to me, for they always gave me their loving care in the early days when I was eight years old and suffered quite severely from asthma, when I had to be treated with lots of penicillin injections; I was not permitted to have any cold drinks or ice-cream and watching my diet was very demanding for them. It also required so much attention to keep my lungs protected and warm. I really made an effort by wearing a protective T-shirt and by taking my medication on time, and trying to exercise, keeping healthy by running, by playing football and other sports with my friends and school mates. It's something that lives with me today but not so much anymore, as I am a strong man today. I still need to take care of my lungs but the struggle is nowhere as serious as it used to be.

Besides, I had a good education and all the attention possible while at school. It was fun all the time as I had everything I needed and I had the privilege of having had the happiest possible childhood; my parents had to adjust and make sacrifices in raising compassionate children, for emotionally we were well balanced, our parents being able to express their true feelings of love towards us. I believe it was all part of the great challenge of bringing up children which must have been difficult for them as their lives were filled with oppression in those days with all the wars and political upheavals they had to live with. In those uncertain times the government policies were different and it was all a matter of adjustment all the time as the traditional methods of teaching were being questioned and altered. Education was being adjusted to the needs of the times as they vacillated between bad times and good times.

My mind goes back in time when I had the chance to wander around the Niassa Game Reserve in northern Mozambique. It was and is one of the most pristine wilderness areas in Africa with a surface area of 42,000 km. It's an important discovery for the tourist with its great concentration of wild life. I really enjoyed the game drives, game walks, rock climbing, and there are people that like hiking and star gazing while thousands of elephants, buffalo and endangered wild dogs roam freely. I saw lions, leopards and a rich diversity of wildlife and birdlife. You get the chance to enjoy safaris, and see the animals that I really enjoyed seeing, like the Johnston's Impala, Boehm's zebra and wildebeest. The highest rock formations in Mozambique are in the Mecula mountain range where you will find the largest protected Miombo forest ecosystems in Mozambique and the world. It's a lovely place to visit if you like safaris.

Crabs are an exciting part of my life as I like to eat them! Their meat is just fine and if properly cooked quite tasty. Back in Tofo Beach where I used to go on Sundays with a family, I loved the sun, ocean water and the place normally is infected with lots of crabs! It's quite fun playing with them, but lots of people are normally terrified of them. How wonderfully rational is that! But there are other deadly things like venomous spiders and great white sharks, whereas crabs are just crabs. They normally are around the beach and people catch them. They run around in the sand and there are lots of sizes; I used to count them and generally had fun doing so.

Gorongosa National Park in Sofala Province is a place I really like, because it is located in the southernmost part of the Great Rift Valley of East Africa. Gorongosa lies between the cities of Chimoio and Beira, and is Mozambique's national flagship as a conservation area. Gorongosa is easily accessible by road and is situated just off the main north-south motorway, close to Inchope junction, and the ecology and history of the park are fascinating. It is one of the great conservation undertakings in the world today and I have seen so much diversity of species there, as it is home to a significant population of oribi, reedbuck, waterbuck, warthog and sable with large herds of the latter up to 110 animals per herd. The warthog are more common than the impala, while there are lots of lion and other predators; elephant herds and bulls are to be seen a lot, too. There must be lots of bird species, maybe around 130 species in an amazing variety. I found this park to be a really exceptional experience.

I have had a chance to learn some of the local languages and the Tonga people live in Inhambane Province of Southeast Mozambique, from Inhambane south to Morrumbene; as the Bantu-speaking people they share the general history of migration from central Europe which began around the time of Christ, and there are Tonga people in Zambia and Zimbabwe. There are Tonga groups that speak dialects such as Ndau in Mozambique and Tumbuka in Zambia and Tanzania and there are neighbours to Tsonga also called Shangaan as well. I used to have fun trying to speak the languages of the local people.

Chapter Thirty

• • •

HOW DO WE DESCRIBE HAPPINESS? I find the most important thing is to have a primary goal in life, and setting out to achieve that goal brings a sense of fulfilment; whatever you are trying to be or achieve, inner peace, holistic health, contentment, inner joy, it's the striving towards that goal that gives purpose to your life. Happiness will be compounded if you can realise your dreams, or desires, in the process overcoming challenges. I do like to feel successful, and it's great if in achieving success you can make a meaningful contribution to the world's needs as well as your own. Like everything, life takes its course, but with perseverance you can shape your destiny.

I have lived in England for so long now, fulfilling my goal to run a successful curry house, and this has given me great satisfaction. The curry house lifestyle has always been on the top on my list of goals, and as I run a curry house, it's good to talk about the hot dishes like chicken madras and chicken vindaloo that are so flavoured and so hot to eat, yet so loved by the local people. It gives me great satisfaction to see their enjoyment of these dishes. I sell lots of different types, like the curry (medium), *dupiaza* (fried onions), *rogan josh* (tomato based), *bhuna* (fairly dry style), *balti* (sweet and sour taste), *jeera* (cumin seed), ginger (chopped ginger), garlic (garlic flavour) and many of today's popular dishes like the chicken tikka massala and chicken korma, which are the most famous and popular that I sell in the restaurant; there are other, innovative dishes, of course, that I like to conjure up for individual needs. It's an exciting world in its own right and I have been involved in it a long time.

As you may well have guessed, I am an admirer of food and back in the land of Inhambane I love to eat the tiger prawns, grilled or fried; but the piri piri prawns are what I really love and enjoy either with beer or wine. It's a cuisine left behind by the Portuguese and to this day everyone loves the dish and it's important to know how to please the customer and a friend for a treat. I have come across some of the best sized prawns and piri piri in Inhambane, and to do justice to them in the preparation of the dish, chillies are mixed with garlic, fresh lemon, oil, and grilled on a nice hot grill. The marinade takes time but it's well worth it. It's much nicer with the head, shell and the tail, as you can kind of enjoy the sources on them. When well prepared and fried or grilled, it's just the business! The way I love them is with a cup of olive oil, 10 fresh chilli peppers, cleaned and chopped, 1 large onion, minced juice from a few fresh limes or lemons, 1 entire bulb of garlic shelled and chopped fine, 1 cup of fresh flat leaf parsley well chopped, 2 spoons of salt and 4 spoons of paprika. All this must be mixed in a bowl and left for some time as needed, and when mixed properly it then goes on to the cooking process; and you know, as it gets ready, I just don't have the words to describe the aroma! It's so nice to eat. Without doubt it's my favourite dish!

A strong person like me knows how to keep his life in order, but even with tears in my eyes I still manage to say I am okay, with a smile every time. Maybe life is what you make it!

My roots being in Southern Africa, I have always loved wine and we have lots of choices in our land, like the very famous wines we have today originating from Africa and the world at large. I like to go to sample tasting of the wines and sangrias served in the wine tent, and like pinotage, shiraz, sauvignon blanc and chardonnay; every year there are festivals in Southern Africa and it's important for me, being a wine lover, to frequent these sort of functions.

As I said, I seem to come across many types of prawns like black tiger prawns, white prawns, flower prawns, large prawns, live scampi, king prawns, shrimps, lobsters, crabs, cuttlefish, Mozambique wild prawns, langoustines and head-on-banana prawns——and there are many more out there that I have not tried.

Like so many fans out there, I am a fan of water sports and I have come across some of the representatives of the bloodthirsty predator called the shark! It's a worry when you're swimming just off a quiet side of the beach and maybe kite-surfing. Maybe it's your presence that attracts these denizens of the deep, and even the smallest looks from one of them is intimidating when near you! These predators are the masters of the deep waters, but only a threat when they are hungry; and I came to know that there are only three types of sharks that are a real danger to humans––the bull, tiger and the great white shark, but even so the attacks are rare. It's nice to see them in real life.

CHAPTER THIRTY-ONE

. . .

HOW MY MIND keeps going back to those paradise islands in Mozambique! Indeed, in my imagination I always end up there, and they are paradise islands for love birds; as I said before, the place lives on in me and is the most exciting 'adventure module' that makes me feel as though washed up on deserted islands where, if I stayed on——on the beaches or in any of the luxury cabins——I would be in a perpetual state of bliss! As my mind takes me back there, I can see myself in a cabin with a private outdoor shower! It's always a joy to be there and most of the time I love a bit of wine, fresh fruit and, as I said before, calamari or the best shrimps I have ever tasted; and from time to time I love to go snorkelling amongst the brightly coloured fish that you usually see in an aquarium. One can just laze about on the beaches, or head out on a sailboat to see a bit of the sun sinking into the distant sea. It is the ideal romantic setting for honeymoon goers. From the comfort of a lazy beach-chair by the pool, I love to gaze across the blue water of the ocean, seeing the sailing boats on the water, and just relax, watching everything around me. Satisfied and quite relaxed on my paradise island––maybe that's me!

It all comes back to me as I was born in Mozambique. I find that the country has left its shattering past behind. Today those living there or those implicated in it are rebuilding the country for a better future. It is going forward at a remarkable pace, and as I have illustrated, there is plenty to see, like the beaches and the islands being a world heritage site, and the charming colonial architecture and colourful local culture. As I said, I find that the best time to visit the country is between May and November, but it's fine to go whenever you can make it.

As I learned in my school time, the first people to see Mozambique's Indian ocean sunrises were small, scattered clans of nomads who were likely trekking through the bush as early as 10,000 years ago; but the real story begins around 3000 years ago, when the Bantu people began migrating into the distant Niger Delta, bringing iron tools and weapons with them. Then scattered kingdoms began to arise including the Karanga or Shona, which extended from present-day Zimbabwe into Mozambique, and the legendary kingdom of Monomotapa near Tete. Meanwhile from around the 8th century AD, sailors from Arabia began to arrive along the coast. One of the most important trading posts was Sofala, near present-day Beira, which by the 15th century was the main link connecting Kilwa with the island gold fields. Other early coastal ports were the island of Mozambique, Angoche, Quelimane and the island of Ibo, ruled by local sultans until Vasco da Gama sailed into the scene in 1498. Over the following centuries the Portuguese built forts and set up trading points along the coast and by the mid-16th century ivory had replaced gold as the main trading commodity; and by 18th-century slaves had been added to the list.

In modern times, in the early 20th century expansion of the nearby gold mines, oppressive Portuguese labour laws led to a mass labour migration from southern Mozambique to South Africa and the old Rhodesia. Mozambicans who had had enough of exploitation caused the resistance movement to grow and in 1964, shots fired in the village of Chai set off the struggle that finally culminated in the independence of the country in 1975. Today it is counted as Africa's best rising star in the constellation of countries in Africa.

One of the things I love is kite-surfing and my land of Mozambique provides constant adventure for kite-surfers. The dirt roads, mud, tropical vegetation, wildlife, is all part of the wider package of adventure offered by the country—and Inhambane is the *pièce de résistance* with its beautiful palm lined beaches, white sands edged by a sea that is so blue, with dozens of quality waves. It is truly a paradise for lovers of this sort of sport. The wind and the surf are perfect for it, the water temperature normally being warm, though it might be a good idea to bring a wet suit. I love the experience, all in keeping with the true pulse and rhythm of Africa.

I am so suited to Mozambique, for apart from having been born in this beautiful land, 1 embody its beautiful and diverse culture, for there is a lot of diversity in my Indian background with its various, merging cultures, where traditions and religion are manifest in rituals that we have to follow. Mozambique encompasses an entire way of life. How indeed do you define your culture when it encompasses such a complex diversity? Mostly it partakes of the Indian lifestyle, quite complex in the way we live, dress, talk, decorate, worship, go to festivals, and in the way we look and eat, express our sincere religious feelings and speak so many different languages. It all comes together in its own unique way, which is our Indian heritage.

Now in the 21st century, the Indian people and population are rapidly becoming quite the largest consumer market in the world, with a middle class growing over half a billion, though millions are still desperately poor, illiterate, with violence still widespread, with lots of corruption in evidence: brides tortured, and poverty, above all, makes it hard for everyone; but the merging of modernity and tradition is making a way for change, opening the way to new and modern ideas and technology. Still, with a conservative society in general dictating the pace of change, things are moving in the direction of a modern democracy.

The Indian ways normally do influence me quite a lot, but then it's all about adjusting to what is happening around me, for I have to say when I look around me today I like the modern world of furniture, fashion, jewellery, tourism, food, beauty, software, hardware, culture, art, craft---you just name it, it's all part of the changing modern scene. It's inevitable that an Indian should become caught up and involved, somehow, with modernity; nevertheless, with our rich Indian heritage there are too many reasons not to be proud to be an Indian no matter how much the world has changed.

In one day so many things happen to us and I find that by trying a new angle things do get better and you can experience new ways and ideas; but I always come to terms with life by making adjustments and trying to have a better day at the same time; for example, when I get up I have to clean myself and then look for breakfast; serious matters might begin with a single letter and bill, and then before you know it, you're off again, through the door, plunged into the world of reality once again, going to work, perhaps driving to work. It all gets very interesting once you are at work, experiencing the way each challenge is resolved or sorts itself out; once again it is decision time, for like everyone else in the working world, decisions are the staple ingredients of the day. The decisions that confront me in my daily life are enjoyable because my life has been the restaurant business for so long that I just like to talk about food, and food, and food, again, again, and again!

Say you run a restaurant––consider, then, how polite you have to be to the customers and keep smiling and smiling! I just do that all the time, and it's fun talking to people and serving them with appetising Indian food, as we do. I find that the Indian restaurant trade is quite interesting because you get a chance to eat spicy food, and I love eating all the spicy food of the world, especially when you have to provide the hot and spicy dishes like we serve in the Indian restaurants over and over again. It's a unique lifestyle and is accompanied by all the interesting touches that are behind (or part of!) the scene, like the music and the décor, and the requirement that the Indian staff should always be smartly dressed. I find the background music quite captivating to listen to and feel that it creates a very pleasant, calm atmosphere that is part of the dining experience you are selling. It's all about providing good food in a nice atmosphere.

Chapter Thirty-Two

• • •

INDIAN JEWELLERY is something that is part of my life as well, as my wife loves wearing it. I think it's all to do with fashion and style, where the right kind of jewellery needs to be worn for the right occasion. She loves going to the social gatherings where all my family or friends are gathered together, and enjoys a day out somewhere to participate in someone's festive day; it's so lovely to see her sometimes with anklets complemented by semi-precious gemstones, or bracelets in sterling silver, normally the perfect ornament to adorn her wrist; then, looking at her earrings––wow! They are sometimes gold or designer silver or just imitation. There are so many types of jewellery she loves to wear, and always looks first class whatever she wears––gold jewellery in Indian ethnic designs, mostly featuring 22 and 18 karat, or 24 karat, but depending on the occasion and looks as well, she loves the necklaces and here, again, there are so many kinds of these, with semi-precious gemstones, gold, silver designs, etc. Mostly they are pre-designed sets, some with pearls and others with pendants, but I mostly love the rings. I have worn rings, too, as a gift with nice designs to them. I think jewellery, with all its diversity, is an interesting world.

Talking about jewellery and my wife's love of wearing it, my thoughts turn to the fact that Indian jewellery is all linked to the Indian world with its celebrations like weddings; there are numerous occasions, in fact, when a woman receives a gift of jewellery, as from her parents and relatives, for safekeeping and to be worn as ornamentation. The cities across India have shops full of jewellery, some traditional and some modern, catering for the needs of all kinds, with a choice ranging from low cost jewellery for low income groups to expensive items for the well-to-do families. Indian houses have various kinds of jewellery, ranging from *Meenakari* and *Kundan* to stone and beadwork. The craft of cutting and polishing precious and semi-precious stones and giving them a glamorous face is an artistic skill. Rubies, garnets, emeralds, corals, sapphires, amethysts and turquoises are among the stones which are used for the enhancement of gold and silver jewellery. Gold is the most popular among Indians as it is considered auspicious and a status symbol. It was inspired by the Mughal art of setting precious stones like diamonds, rubies, emeralds in gold or silver jewellery; there are antique jewellery, bead, bridal, custom, fashion, filigree, gold jewellery, handmade, ivory, jadau, kundan, lac, meenakari jewellery, navratna, pachchikam, silver, stone, temple and tribal jewellery. Because there is so much choice when it comes to jewellery in India, the country is a veritable wonderland, an Aladdin's cave, for Indian girls to find and enjoy wearing the jewellery of their choice.

Indian rickshaws is a way of life in India and whenever I travel while on holiday in India I get the chance of riding in one of them to travel around for the daily shopping, or to get from A to B, and it's quite fun wandering around in one of them; but then it's quite economical as well, as each rickshaw only holds eight litres of fuel and travels at a maximum speed of 30mph. I got the chance to visit friends and restaurants, as well as my wife who had a chance of going shopping with me, often riding with me in them. The experience of travelling around in them is quite memorable, and from their vantage point I had the opportunity of seeing at close hand the overpowering Indian crowds, being driven through monsoon rains and sometimes the flooded streets, as well as along balmy coastlines and through misty jungles. I used to ride with local rickshaw drivers that know the way and it's quite a help, as I got to cover so many new areas and distances, seeing places I never thought of seeing or staying in. The rickshaw is essentially a cycle––what could be described as a small-scale form of transport. It's also known as a pedi-cab, bike-cab, cyclo, becak or trishaw, or simply a rickshaw that is pulled by a person on foot; normally they are human powered and it's a type of tricycle designed to carry passengers in addition to the driver and often used on a hire basis. I enjoyed all the rickshaws in Bombay city; nothing is so common in Indian towns and cities as the angry buzz and two-stroke haze of the wheeled auto-rickshaws that normally adorn most of the roads in Bombay and Delhi, the big cities. Human-powered cycle-rickshaws clog the narrow lanes, ferrying passengers and goods of every kind. It's a tourist attraction as well, of course, as it's a way for local rickshaw *wallahs* to make a living and keep the people moving to the destinations required by the needs of individuals. I just love them!!

One of the destinations I love in India is the palm-fringed Goa beaches. These beaches constitute some of the most famous tourist places I know, and are the popular haunts of many people. The beach life of villages like Benaulim is often an uneasy balance between tourism and traditional activity. The fishing boats of Palolem are almost eclipsed by the overdevelopment of the village and it's known as Paradise Beach. I love the sunrises and sunsets there and the weather is just fantastic. Altogether it is a really good Indian spot that I love, especially as a place to relax in and escape from the hurly-burley of the rat-race!

As I travelled quite often through the chaotic roads full of traffic comprised of the swirling mass of flesh and metal, I felt overwhelmed by the sheer variety of forms of transport which defies belief, like camel carts, bullock carts, cows, elephants and human-powered rickshaws. All of these vie for a position on the roads, with taxis, and maruti cars, overloaded trucks, motorcycles and scooters caught up in a cacophony of horns and the diesel haze––a haze of pollution that engulfs so many of the towns and cities of India.

It's all part of the vibrant life of India, I guess. India's most colourful markets, from Kashmir to Kanyaku Mari, bustle with activity and form the backbone of India's domestic commerce. The market stalls sell everything, from books, flowers and clothes to fruit, vegetables and woven baskets, and most are permanent though some appear seasonally, such as those selling Indian sweets for the Diwali festival. Most people working for a living in India carry out their activities in a more favourable environment than their forbears did in times gone by. Manual labour work is still common and often a backbreaking way to earn a living, and from the fishermen of the south to the shipman, millions of people engage in hard and dangerous labour for a daily wage.

CHAPTER THIRTY-THREE

• • •

LOVE MARRIAGES these days are something we find more and more frequently in today's Indian and African cultures. I think that happy marriages begin when we marry the ones we love, and they say a relationship or marriage blossoms when we love the ones we marry. If one were to try to define a successful marriage, then one might be tempted to use the old romantic cliché in the song that says 'love and marriage go together like a horse and carriage'! I think love is a dream and marriage is an extension of that dream, whereby the dream becomes reality. When it all comes together it's the best thing that happens to an individual, like, perhaps, it has happen to me, as I can testify that it's an emotional wave within us––a feeling that is inexplicable, for the company of the person we love can make a person feel a little bit of that ecstasy and excitement that makes life worth living. In India love marriages are becoming a popular trend these days, while traditional arranged marriages used to be the only option for the boys and girls; but the parents today have a broader perspective and are quite aware of the nuances of the caste system, thanks to the education available these days. Commitment is a big thing, but arranged marriages in many instances are still viewed as the right thing; there are still two sides to be considered, and the drawback of love marriages is the inability to adjust to family members of the person one is marrying into. However, with a little bit of adjustment, it's love marriages that are more successful these days.

There are lots of different types of weddings in India and I learned over the years that Hindu marriages are quite popular; but there are so many in India, like Telugu weddings, Tamil, Sindhi, Punjabi, Oriya, Muslim, Marwari, Malayalee, Maithil Brahmin, Maharashtrian, Kashmiri, Gujurati, Kannada, Jewish, Jain, Buddhist, Bengali, Ssamese, as well as other types of marriages.

The ethnic Indian interior designs are a big inspiration to me because mostly I like to explore the natural terracotta art, and back in India we have a huge collection of terracotta wall hangings, vases, bowls and many similar ideas that I really have a passion for; and the natural earthy and clay look of mud sculptures are made in lots of different forms and shapes and figures, and lots of homes are decorated with wind chimes, pots, decorative accents and many more ideas like painted terracotta. It's the new trend as artists now use colours like green, yellow, red, orange, to give a bright look to the clay, and it brings a fresh look to old walls, as then the ethnic Indian lanterns are widely used around villages to light up, as it's all part of India's best natural art.

Being an Indian, I am aware of Indian customs and Indian ways of doing things. It all starts I think from birth—all the vedic recitations, yoga classes, the breathing techniques, the concentration techniques, as the sage of India is found through deep meditation and various concentration techniques; these make the thoughts so calm and clear, giving the brain its full potential. Breath control makes the body and mind stronger, and knowledge of the truth generates confidence in daily life, and risk-taking is eliminated by proper planning. Indians lay more emphasis on technical knowledge as can be seen in music, science, software development and other areas; and the one big part of an Indian's life is religion, as all the people are very religious and believe in truth and purity. India is the country where major religious days are celebrated, as an expression of real, living faith and for its own reasons.

Clearly, it is this Indian ethos, a way of life that came first from India and which informs the country of my birth, Mozambique, which has inspired me in writing this book. On this note I would like to thank all my readers and my well-wishers who have made this book a unique and memorable experience. My hope is that you will find that it has opened doors in your minds, in your culinary tastes, and in your travels, especially if you should ever visit and explore the terrains of which I have spoken. Thank you, finally, for allowing me to share so much of my life with you!

Printed in the United States
By Bookmasters